YES I CAN

Con Hurley is from Cork. As a young boy he spent a year with his grandparents on their farm in West Cork and acquired a love of the land and people. This was in contrast to East London, where he spent seven years with his parents and four siblings. Returning to Ireland he went to school and university. He then joined the *Irish Farmers Journal* to write on dairy farming for over thirty years. In 2005 he moved to a career in life coaching. Con is enthusiastic about life and helping people to find happiness and fulfilment. He lives with his wife near the village of Union Hall in West Cork where he pursues his hobbies of vegetable gardening, reading and walking.

www.conhurley.com

YES I CAN

ACHIEVE PERSONAL SUCCESS
WITH THE
LIFE PLANNING TOOLKIT

CON HURLEY

The Collins Press

FIRST PUBLISHED IN 2009 BY
The Collins Press
West Link Park
Doughcloyne
Wilton
Cork

British Library Cataloguing in Publication Data
Hurley, Con.
    Yes I can : achieve success with the life-planning
    toolkit.
    1. Lifestyles. 2. Self-evaluation.
    3. Self-actualization (Psychology) 4. Success.
I. Title
158.1-dc22
ISBN-13: 9781848890008

Typesetting by The Collins Press
Typeset in AGaramond 11 pt
Printed in Great Britain by J F Print Ltd

Cover images courtesy of Con Hurley and Tom Moore

DEDICATION AND

ACKNOWLEDGEMENTS

This book is dedicated to you, dear reader, that it may help you on your journey through life.

Yes I Can would never have come into existence – and I might not have been here to write it – without the love and support of my best friend, my partner and guide in life, my wife Eleanor. We have been married for thirty-five years and I'm looking forward to the next thirty-five. I also acknowledge the support from our children: Caroline, Jerry and John.

I thank the friends who have helped me and been part of my journey: John O'Keeffe, Michael Murphy, Lori Fitzgerald, Lynaire Ryan and John Fahy (deceased).

I acknowledge the people who have been part of my professional development. I thank all the staff at the *Irish Farmers Journal*, who helped hone my writing skills. These were further enhanced by David Rice at the Killaloe Hedge-School of Writing. In life coaching, I am grateful for the help and support of Ann Boylan, Bernadette Coleman, Karina Connolly, Julie Silfverberg and Mety Zantingh.

Finally, the people who have helped take this book from a raw manuscript to the finished product: my heartfelt thanks to all the staff at The Collins Press. Then there is Cathy Thompson, who spent many hours editing the manuscript and from whom I've learnt many writing and editing ideas that will serve me in the future. And, finally, Tom Moore, a close friend and a graphic artist. Thanks, Tom, for the illustrations and creative cover.

CONTENTS

PROLOGUE

The central thrust of *Yes I Can* is to help you develop the skills and knowledge that lead to personal success in life. Never is this more relevant than in a time of financial crisis – at such times people become aware of the need to anchor their lives to something firm, something that really matters.

Personal success means different things to different people, but ultimately it is all about happiness. Everybody wants to be happy in life. People may use words like 'success', 'achievement' and 'challenge', but the ultimate goal is happiness. In my experience, happiness follows people who:

- define what is important in their lives;
- focus on these important areas; and
- measure their levels of satisfaction (happiness) in these areas.

I believe that if you use the tools and exercises in the following pages, you will be a happier person. I urge you to do this because I am certain that people who have done so will weather the current recession far better than people who focus mainly on their financial situation.

The reason for this is illuminating. Every person I have encountered who has defined and prioritised their important areas of life has come up with the same results. Every person – and I must have used this exercise with at least 400 people to date. For them the most important areas of life focus on close, loving relationships and health.

I know that people who are highly satisfied with these areas of their lives will come through the recession very well. This is because finance and money are not the most important areas in life. Important, yes – but not as important as relationships and health. So my main message to you is to treat the recession as an opportunity to get real balance into your life. I believe that *Yes I Can* can take you on an exciting journey of self-discovery through these hard times – and that you will emerge a stronger, happier human being.

Part One tells you about my own life journey: the things that worked for me and the things that did not. And, most importantly, the lessons I learnt along the way.

Part Two is where you begin to take control of your own life: this is your opportunity to take responsibility for the way you are living, to make the choices and adopt the attitudes that will take you down the road you want to travel.

Part Three is the heart of the book: here you will find a practical Life Planning Toolkit so that each day you can begin to create the balanced life you want to live. You will learn how to identify and prioritise your important areas of life and set goals that lead to personal success and happiness.

By the time you have finished reading, I sincerely hope that you will already be experiencing the pleasure we all can know when we become drivers rather than simply passengers on our own journey through life.

Con Hurley
Spring 2009

PART ONE:

MY JOURNEY

CHAPTER 1: 'WHAT MAKES ME TICK?'

CHAPTER 2: BEWARE OF EXPERTS

What is Self-knowledge and Why Seek It?

How Can You Gain Self-knowledge?

CHAPTER 3: SELF-DISCOVERY

Depression and Burnout, 1996
  Beyond Prozac

Wealth Creation Course

Strategic Planning
  Mission statements

Life Coaching, 2005
  Career change

CHAPTER 4: YOUR PERSONAL LEARNING JOURNAL

(PLJ Exercise: Self-assessment Process 1: Your LifeTime Chart)

1

CHAPTER 1

'WHAT MAKES ME TICK?'

'I'm going to find out what makes me tick!' That's how it all began on a balmy autumn day in 1996. I was just finishing my seventh session with a psychotherapist. She had looked at me with amazement – and perhaps concern – when I informed her that this was our last session. 'Oh,' she said calmly (I suppose psychiatrists are always calm), 'Why is that?'

I was prepared to give an explanation. 'Well, Doctor, it's like this: I've been coming here for almost three months and I'm now much better than when I came here first. Thank you for that. However, there seems to be a predictable pattern to our sessions. You continue to ask me about my past, especially my parents and childhood. I can tell you that my mother never beat the daylights out of me and my father never raped me. Oh, and I got on well with my brothers and sister. OK, we were broke a few times and we moved a lot. But, basically, we were a very happy family. What's more,' I added with emphasis, 'I don't believe I am repressing any unpleasant or traumatic memories.'

I could see that the learned doctor a little uncomfortable and the next question she asked me was: 'Well, what are you going to do?' And the answer just popped into my head. 'I'm going to find out what makes me tick!' At the time, I did not consciously realise the significance of that statement. It came from somewhere else in my mind – the unconscious, or

3

intuition perhaps. In fact, at that stage, I knew little or nothing about intuition or unconscious minds. That came later.

When I had first visited my GP earlier that same summer of 1996, I had known I was in trouble, probably on the verge of a nervous breakdown. I had had a few problems during the previous eighteen months, but nothing as bad as the feelings that had led to that visit. On previous occasions I had felt a bit 'down', lacking in energy and suffering from dull headaches and pains in my shoulders and upper arms. I had been in hospital and been checked out for 'everything'. On one occasion, a specialist physiologist had told me that I was perfect, absolutely nothing wrong with me. 'You're the healthiest man in Cork,' he told me with a smile. 'If that's the case,' I responded, 'how is it that I feel so bad?' No response. I suppose, like all the specialists I encountered at that time, he dealt only with his own speciality. As far as he and his speciality were concerned, I was fine.

Anyway, things were definitely going from bad to worse in the summer of 1996. Looking back, I think it was a build-up of all the stressful situations I had gone through during the previous few years. The main source of stress was, I believe, my job. I worked as dairy editor for the *Irish Farmers Journal*. Overall, this was a wonderful career and involved plenty of travel, speaking engagements, and writing technical articles about the science and practice of profitable, efficient milk production. I was very good at what I did. The *Journal*, as it is popularly known, comes out weekly and I worked to three deadlines for different pages. I regarded this as normal.

I aimed to provide cutting-edge information and leadership for dairy farmers and I always tried to act in the best interests of my main readers – ordinary people trying to make a living for themselves and their families. I attacked my job with missionary zeal. I was on their side 100 per cent and this often led to conflict with advisors, researchers, co-ops, marketing agencies and farming politicians. If what they were saying or selling was not in the best interest of my audience, I took them all on with gusto, believing and *knowing* that I was doing the right thing for farmers. Maybe I was – but was I doing the right thing for Con Hurley?

I did not know it at the time, but I was walking towards a mental cliff. Aside from the stressful job, there were other problems in my life. Our house move in 1995 was complicated by all kinds of legal and financial problems. Then my father was diagnosed with cancer and was dying. I coped with all that – or so I thought. But the stress levels were building up. The tipping point, the straw that broke the camel's back, came on a lovely summer's day in 1996 – a Tuesday – when I was writing frantically to meet a deadline. It was only a small thing that tipped the balance – in the middle of the rush to meet my deadline there was a phone call from a very irate farmer-reader. He had misinterpreted some advice I had published the previous week – with unwanted results for his cattle. It was not the end of the world, but for some reason it had a huge effect on me. It pushed me over the cliff edge. I could feel the panic surging in; it was almost physical. Wow, as I write this now I can still feel it in my gut and I wonder how I got through it all. Well, of course, I did not. I cracked up in that summer. Complete burnout.

I had enough presence of mind to write down how I was feeling and Eleanor, my wife, took me to see my GP. He did not examine me physically. There was no need. He read my note of self-diagnosis and said, 'Con, I'd like you to see a psychiatrist. Would you agree to that?' My response was emphatic. 'Look Paddy, if you told me there was a witch-doctor in the Congo who could cure me, I'd be on the first plane into the jungle!'

The appointment was made and I went to see Dr X, a

lovely lady. We got on well and, at the end of our first session, she told me I had depression. She advised me to take three months off work and prescribed a course of antidepressants for me. Relief flooded in – I did not have to go back to work for three months and there was a definite diagnosis. Within ten days the antidepressants took effect and I began to feel much better. The pains eased and the pall that seemed to cover my head began to evaporate. I began to feel well again. Well enough to want to do things, rather than sitting around the house all day or staying in bed. So I did three things that have enriched my life: I learnt how to type; I learnt how to use a computer; and I rejoined the library after an absence of some thirty years. I did not know it at the time, but these events launched me on the most interesting phase and journey of my life – and believe me, I had already been on some memorable journeys in my life and career.

I have always been a voracious reader. For me, books are a ready source of both information and enjoyment. When I was about ten years old, my parents bought an encyclopaedia called *The Books of Knowledge* and I devoured the information in these wonderful volumes. At school and university I was always very curious, reading widely and eagerly, and lapping up new facts and information. When I started work as a dairy editor my job involved reading press releases, reports and research papers. I learnt how to access and analyse information from many sources.

So it was only natural that my appetite for information would lead me to find out more about depression. What was it? How could it be cured? These were the main questions. Of course, I could have just accepted Dr X's assurance that continuing psychotherapy and antidepressants would cure me, but she was unable to say how long that would take. I could have become a passive patient, dependent on the expert for my health. But no, I wanted to be involved. I wanted to know all about depression, what caused it, and how I could get rid of it.

I sought knowledge – and where better to find it than in books? When I walked back into Cork City Library, a limestone-faced building on the Grand Parade, I felt as if I was going home. With all the ships of knowledge sitting on the shelves, waiting to be boarded and explored, it was a safe haven for my disturbed, but still curious, mind. There were books about depression, psychology, stress and psychiatrists. I read about Freud and Adler, psychoanalysis and psychotherapy, cognitive therapy – and how depression is caused and treated. And I learnt a lot about the methods that the medical and psychiatric establishment used to diagnose and treat mental illness and depression. I bought into the theory that depression is caused by an imbalance of chemicals in the brain and that the cure is a combination of antidepressants and psychotherapy.

This exploration ensured that I was happy with Dr X – for a while. The pills were working and I enjoyed our one-hour sessions in the comfortable leather armchair and the pleasant surroundings of her room. But as the sessions progressed and I learnt more from my reading, I came to the conclusion that the therapy she was using was based on Freudian thinking. Sigmund Freud founded the psychoanalytic school of psychology. He believed that the root causes of most mental illness could be traced back to the repression of traumatic childhood experiences – and that these were often sexual in nature, since he also believed that sexual desire was the main motivating energy for human beings.

From this knowledge, I began to realise that Dr X was looking for experiences in my childhood that would explain her diagnosis of depression. When I finally left Dr X in 1996, I was just happy to be feeling better mentally and physically. The medication was working, but I rejected Freudian-based psychotherapy. To be fair to Dr X, in her initial diagnostic session she had spent a long time asking me about my work and life. And she had also pointed out that I was working eighty hours a week and was a perfectionist. There was mention of stress, too. Looking back, I believe that if she had focused on solving these issues, I might have stayed with her longer.

I believe this is true because, strangely enough, these were exactly the areas I tackled in order to discover what makes me 'tick'. During that period the book that helped me most was called *Stress Management*, written in 1982 by two American doctors, Edward Charlesworth and Ronald Nathan. Although it has been in print for a while, most of the information is still very relevant today. The book's subtitle is 'A comprehensive guide to wellness' and the cover blurb on my copy tells the reader that this is 'the one book you should read if you feel under pressure'.

Well, I read it and I took what I wanted and really needed at the time – in particular assertive time management, as it related to my work. And I acted on the information, taking the following steps:

1. I made a list of the things that an excellent (not perfect) dairy editor must do.

2. I said 'no' to any other job-related activity that was not on this list.

I was surprised at how easy it was to make my list, but found that saying 'no' proved more challenging. The 'excellent editor' list included:

- keeping abreast of the latest research;

- staying in touch with leading farmers and advisors;

- ensuring clarity over what should be included in each column;

- focusing on reader requirements;

- maintaining a clear, easy-to-understand, writing style;

- meeting deadlines; and

- planning ahead for articles.

Then I looked back and reviewed how I had been allocating my time: eighty hours a week over the previous two to three years. Two things stuck out like sore thumbs: unnecessary travel and speaking engagements. I loved both speaking and travelling and they often went together. In one year, I estimated that I had made over forty presentations at different meetings all over Ireland and in New Zealand, the UK and France. It certainly helped my work as a dairy editor, but this aspect of my career was not essential. It was not on the 'excellent editor' list. In reality it was an ego trip.

That exercise was a real eye-opener. It showed me what I needed to focus on to be an excellent editor and to provide high-quality information to my readers. And it identified exactly where I was spending time in unnecessary work, so I decided to cut this out. That took commitment. You see, if you have a reputation as a 'giver', then people expect you to continue giving and they will never stop asking. I had a reputation as a good speaker and I always said 'yes'. The word was, 'If you need a speaker for a seminar or conference, ask Con Hurley.'

When I returned to work, people continued asking me to speak. But Charlesworth and Nathan are very clear that we all have inalienable rights: 'You have the right to refuse a request. In fact, you have the right to say "no" to any request without feeling guilty.' So I knew I had to begin to refuse speaking engagements if I was to reduce my workload from eighty to fifty hours or less per week. I explained my situation to people and most accepted my reasons. A few persisted and eventually gave up – and finally the word went out that Con Hurley was no longer available for speaking.

And that was it: the world kept turning, the sun did not fall from the sky, the cows were still milked and the dairy articles still got written. For a while, my sense of self-importance, my ego, suffered. I got over that and, moving into 1997, I was no longer working weekends to prepare speeches and catch up on essential work. There were huge paybacks: my work as dairy editor probably improved; stress levels dropped dramatically; I had more time for Eleanor and our family; and I had time to pursue the mission I had mentioned to Dr X – to find out what makes me tick.

In the next chapter I'm going to tell you what I did on my journey of self-discovery. However, before I move on, I want to emphasise the crucial importance of the time-review exercise and cutting out non-essential activities by saying 'no'. I will come back to this in more detail in Chapter 14. For now, I just want to make it clear that my journey of self-discovery could not have happened if I had not made the time available. The two keys to time management – or, as I prefer to call it, LifeTime Management – are:

1. Identify what is really important and then allocate your lifetime to it.

2. Say 'no' to what is not important.

My career as dairy editor was important, so I gave it the necessary time to do an excellent job – but no more. As a result of my time review or audit, I cut out the unimportant things in my career and, in 1997, was able to allocate time to the challenging and exciting quest for self-knowledge. I was going to find out what makes me tick.

CHAPTER 2

BEWARE OF EXPERTS

ARE YOU AN EXPERT IN SOMETHING, CON, OR WHAT?

(TREVOR JONES)

A few years ago, when I was switching to a new career in life coaching (I'll tell you about that later) I visited an old Welsh friend who was quite ill. As I sat by his bedside in St Clears near Carmarthen, Trevor Jones told me that he had heard I was becoming some sort of consultant or counsellor. Not a man for beating around the bush, he came straight to the point and asked me the question that introduces this chapter. Now Trevor had a PhD in grassland management and was widely regarded as an expert in his field – by everyone except himself. He was a rebel with a thirst for knowledge and was always open to, and eager to embrace, new ideas and thinking. He was suspicious of closed thinking, blueprints and fixed positions – the so-called 'experts'.

I explained to Trevor how life coaching worked and how I dealt with clients and the people who attended my courses in Personal Life Planning and Personal Financial Planning. He was very relieved to hear that I was not putting myself forward as an expert and he gave me a quote that he got from his father: 'Follow the person who seeks the truth, but beware of the bugger who claims to have found it!'

I want to be clear from the outset: I am not putting myself

forward as an 'expert'. In every sense, I am a seeker of truth and knowledge, and specifically knowledge about myself. The questions I am asking are:

- Who am I?

- What do I want in life?

- What is my purpose in life?

These are fundamental human questions that we all have to ask on our personal journeys of self-discovery. And I'm hoping to share with you some of my experiences on my own exciting, challenging, ongoing, and continuous journey. My objectives are to:

1. convince you that there is a huge payback in acquiring self-knowledge;

2. provide you with some tools to get started, and

3. encourage you to commit to a life-long journey of self-discovery.

In fact, whether you know it or not, you are already on this journey. The tragedy for most people is that their life journey is a happy-go-lucky, come-day-go-day, aimless experience. Very few humans have a reasonable understanding of themselves and what they want in life. This was beautifully summed up in a quote attributed to American journalist, Sydney J. Harris: 'Ninety per cent of the world's woe comes from people not knowing themselves, their abilities, their frailties, and even their real virtues. *Most of us go almost all the way through life as complete strangers to ourselves* [my italics].'

In essence, most of us do not really know ourselves. We are 'strangers to ourselves'. With poor self-knowledge, we drift through life marching to the tunes of others without ever recognising and living the vast talent and possibility that dwells within us. What a waste of human potential! We could go further and say that most of us know more about other people than we do about ourselves, but the payback for gaining self-knowledge is immense. Ultimately it leads to a life full of meaning and purpose, fulfilment, happiness and peace of mind.

What is Self-Knowledge and Why Seek It?

In my opinion, self-knowledge means:

- describing who I am physically, mentally and spiritually – my **identity**;

- knowing what's really important to me in life – also my **identity**;

- doing the best I can with what is really important to me – achieving a measure of **success**;

- discovering my ultimate **purpose** in life;

- identifying and achieving goals that allow me to live my life with happiness, meaning and success – creating my **life plan**.

Human beings are a complex mix of very individual character-istics – physical, mental and spiritual. It is therefore clear that no two human beings will have exactly the same sense of identity, purpose or success. But self-knowledge empowers each one of us as individuals – it is about knowing what makes our *own* life meaningful, fulfilling and happy. Once a person has this knowledge, he or she is powerfully enabled to choose the decisions and actions that will create the life he or she wants.

In practice, many, if not most, people rely on circumstances and others to determine how they live their lives. How many of us live our lives based on the advice and opinions of others? We listen to politicians, church leaders, consultants, accountants, bank managers, and other 'experts' as a matter of course, and we also rely heavily on the media – especially TV and newspapers – and advertising. We allow these outside 'experts' and influences to determine how we live our lives. Of course, it is often useful and desirable to get information and opinions from various sources. But, at the end of the day, you will have a happier more meaningful life if you choose how to live based on a growing knowledge of self.

This is well illustrated by an old story about the Delphic Oracle in Ancient Greece. Kings, rich men and other important people who wanted advice travelled to Delphi before making important decisions, since a wise Oracle (Pythia, the Priestess of Apollo) and her retinue of acolytes resided in the sanctuary there. The person seeking advice and guidance (it was usually a man) would present his question to the acolytes, who would then bring it to the Priestess in the inner chamber. The Oracle would go into a trance and deliver her 'inspired' advice, which was written down by an acolyte. The advice was written in such a way that whatever the recipient did, it always looked right – much like the horoscopes that we see in the papers today.

However, the Priestess always told her visitors that the fundamental answer to all their questions and the best advice she could give was written on the arch at the entrance to the her sanctuary. And, as they departed and looked up at the arch, they saw just two words: 'Know Thyself'. I believe that this advice is as good today as it was 2,500 years ago.

How Can You Gain Self-Knowledge?

This is the tricky bit! As I said at the outset, I am not an expert and I do not believe in blueprints, therefore I do not have a 'one-size-fits-all' approach to self-knowledge. That's because I believe that each of us learns differently. Some people find it easy to describe their character traits, values, needs, wants, and so on, but others need to work through exercises and questions to get answers. Time and experience are also very important. The forty-year-old is in a far better position to seek self-knowledge than the teenager.

For many people, the motivation comes from a crisis in life: losing a job, retirement, financial problems, relationship problems, marital strife, death in the family, physical disease and, like me, stress-related mental health problems.

My strong advice is that you should not wait for the crisis. Make a considered choice to get to know yourself deeply now. It has been said that the most difficult thing in life is to know yourself – in fact many people end up knowing more about other people than they do about themselves. So commit. Make it a key goal. Remember what Socrates said: 'The unexamined life is not worth living.' That sounds a bit harsh and very negative, so let's replace it with a positive statement of my own: 'The person who commits to self-knowledge lives a life full of hope, richness, meaning, happiness and peace of mind.'

So where can you start? Well, what I intend to do is to describe my own journey, complete with cul-de-sacs and frustrations, but as you read you will see that it has led to a better quality of life, financial freedom (almost), increased happiness and peace of mind.

When you have read my story, we'll go on to look at steps you can take to begin this journey of self-knowledge yourself and move your own life to another level. You will discover the hidden, unique talents within you – every human being has them. Once uncovered, it is up to you to make the most of these talents for your own benefit and the benefit of society. You will be happier working and living in harmony with your uniqueness. As the saying goes: 'Don't die with the music still in you.'

CHAPTER 3

SELF-DISCOVERY

. . . THE MOMENT ONE DEFINITELY COMMITS ONESELF, THEN
PROVIDENCE MOVES TOO . . .

(W. H. MURRAY, *THE SCOTTISH HIMALAYAN EXPEDITION*)

In 2007 I drafted an outline of this book with all the chapters
and topics clearly identified in advance. That's the logical way
to do it. But it did not feel right. It seemed too formal and
academic, and it gave the impression that life planning and self-
discovery are orderly, step-by-step processes, like making a car
or building a house.

Real life is not that simple. It cannot be defined and lived
according to a strategic plan. Except for one vital component –
knowing what you want in life. Remember that thirteen years
ago I wanted only one thing: to find out what made me 'tick'.
In other words I was on the path to self-knowledge. The steps
I have taken to acquire my current understanding of myself were
not planned in advance. I did not know enough about life
planning to think out the steps I should take.

I am now going to describe the experiences and important
personal discoveries that have opened up my life since 1996. As
we have seen, I started with psychology and how the mind
works – this, at the time, was the most logical starting point.
But one thing led to another. This book is not intended as a

blueprint – I am writing it the way it happened. If I knew then what I know now, I would have taken a different approach, using some of the tools, skills and techniques I describe in later chapters.

Depression and Burnout, 1996

When I was diagnosed with depression it came as a complete shock. It was a personal crisis. But in a strange way, I welcomed that diagnosis as a wake-up call and, looking back now, I see it as a stroke of luck. Deep down I knew that something was wrong with my life. So the diagnosis came as a relief: at last, I had found out what was wrong with me. At the time I was also relieved that I could step back for three months from what had become a very stressful work situation. No more deadlines, no more hassle.

As I explained in Chapter 1, I became unhappy with the type of psychotherapy Dr X used. I was also extremely unhappy and uncomfortable at the thought of becoming dependent. Dependent on antidepressant drugs. Dependent on psychotherapy. This was a very important piece of self-knowledge: I valued independence. In order to make independence real in my life, I needed to take responsibility for getting better.

It would have been tempting to sit back, accept Dr X's brand of psychotherapy, and relax in the carefree feeling I was getting from the antidepressants and the time out of work. If I hit a little downer, as I inevitably would, I could have simply popped a few more pills and all would have been well again. But something inside me would not allow me to accept this dependence on therapy and drugs. I felt very uncomfortable and I rebelled. Although I did not know it at the time, I was coming face to face with my own value system and two of my most strongly held values – independence and responsibility. (See Chapter 5 for more on **responsibility** and Chapter 15 for **values.**)

So what did I do? Well, knowledge is power and I gained both by reading about psychology and psychiatry. This gave me the confidence to discontinue Dr X's psychotherapy. But, as my German neighbour Axel says, 'Get me right': I was still very unwell. I returned to Dr X a few times and I remained on anti-depressants for almost four years.

After three months, I went back to work in a more focused way and began to look for ways of regaining mental health without drugs and psychotherapy. I continued to improve my understanding of how the human brain works by reading widely. This study was prompted by the accepted wisdom that depression is caused by a chemical imbalance in the brain, so it was logical to seek out more information.

I also attended a few group meetings on depression but did not find them very useful. The prevailing thinking seemed to me to be very negative. The focus was on problems. I wanted solutions, but I was finding it difficult to get any. Realistically, I could see that although I had stabilised my work and cut back hugely on unnecessary work-related commitments, I was still on the antidepressants. Then two things happened to help me take full responsibility for my life and gain more control over my future: firstly, I saw a business opportunity to help people plan their lives; and secondly, I met a doctor with a very practical and human approach to mental illness. I'll tell you about him first.

Beyond Prozac

One day I was rummaging through a table of general self-help books in Waterstone's bookshop on Patrick Street, Cork, and I picked up a book called *Beyond Prozac*. What a revelation this proved to be. I read it quickly – and then I read it again. The author, Dr Terry Lynch, provided solid logical reasons that supported my feelings of unhappiness and discomfort about my diagnosis and the therapeutic basis for my sessions with Dr X. He debunked a lot of the mystery about mental illness and our over-dependence on drugs.

I assumed that I had depression because that was the professional diagnosis. But when I saw how the diagnosis was made, I was both indignant and relieved. Dr Lynch quoted the standard method of diagnosis – eight criteria put together by panels of psychiatrists convened by the American Psychiatric Association. I will not list them here, but Dr Lynch's comment on their content is: 'Judge for yourself whether these criteria are scientific, or whether they are merely descriptions of under-standable human feelings and behaviours.'

There are no blood tests for chemical imbalances in the brain, nor is there another objective way of diagnosing depression: just eight criteria, which are totally subjective. I read them once – and then twice – before I realised that, even using these subjective criteria, I should not have been diagnosed with depression in the first place. Somewhere else in the book, I discovered that my symptoms reflected high exposure to stress. Great: that was something I could begin to solve myself.

I was still on antidepressants, but Dr X had told me that these were not addictive. Fine, I was not suffering from depression, so I thought I could give them up. I stopped taking them and – wham! – massive withdrawal symptoms kicked in. I was back on the pills again. As luck would have it, Terry Lynch lived and worked in Limerick, just over an hour's drive from me. So I went to see him as a patient and he helped me wean myself off the antidepressants and supported me in the steps I was taking to regain control over my life and future.

If you, or anyone you know, have been diagnosed with

'mental illness' of any kind and have been prescribed antidepressants, I urge you to read *Beyond Prozac*. It may literally save
your life.

Wealth Creation Course

My contact with Terry Lynch and his wonderful book coincided
with the development of my business idea, which grew from
my insights while dealing with profitable farmers. Although
these farmers were good at making money from farming, they
were pretty poor at managing the money they made. (I now
know that this observation applies not just to farmers, but to
many of us.) I had noticed a pattern in the 1970s, during a
period of high agricultural prices and industry expansion. Some
serious money was made – and most of it was misspent on
expensive land and unnecessary buildings and equipment.
When the downturn came, the result was a lot of heartache and
financial problems for farm families. The profits in the good
times were invested poorly and there was nothing in the kitty
when the hard times came around, as they inevitably do. By the
late 1990s I could see this cycle beginning to repeat itself. And
I wondered what I could do.

Then one beautiful sunny day I was walking in the Caha
Mountains that straddle the border of Counties Cork and
Kerry. I was on my own, enjoying the fresh air and scenery,
when, out of the blue, a thought jumped into my head: what
about a course to train farmers on money management? I
thought it would be a good idea and so I contacted Michael
Murphy, a very successful Cork-based dairy farmer and investor.
As well as being a good friend, he also had a proven track record
in 'wealth creation'. And that's where we got the name 'Wealth
Creation Course'.

We needed help to develop the course, so we contacted two

New Zealanders, Lynaire Ryan and Leonie Foster, both very successful agricultural consultants. We held our first WCC in the autumn and winter of 1998–9. It took place in a small hotel, picturesquely located on the River Shannon in Tipperary, and ran for 8 two-day modules over a three-month period. We developed the content from week to week, often chasing our tails and improvising when we needed to fill an hour or so.

Obviously the main focus of the Wealth Creation Course was money, but as we moved into it I became increasingly uneasy that we were going to end up with twenty raving capitalists – so the four of us considered what we could do to make the course more balanced. In the interim between the first course and WCC2, a year later, we tried a number of approaches and presenters in personal development: a well-known psychiatrist, a 'motivator', and a man with a franchise for an international goal-achievement programme.

None of the approaches worked to our satisfaction. Something was missing. Looking back, I think that these well-meaning people were perhaps full of the theory but lacking in the practice of the programme we were trying to communicate. Get me right, they meant well, but it did not work for most of the participants on our course. And I fell into the same trap when I tried my hand at some 'personal development stuff'.

Around this time I read Stephen Covey's book, *The 7 Habits of Highly Effective People*, and I was bowled over by some of his powerful messages. In particular the book copper-fastened my growing awareness that only I can take responsibility for *my* decisions. Covey covers this in his sections on proactivity, or what he calls 'freedom to choose versus determinism'. And I loved his approach to goal-setting and planning: 'Begin with the end in mind.'

'Wow,' I thought, 'this is the answer. This is what our participants need.' So I put together a series of slides and made a presentation. Was it good? Was it great? Mmm! I do not think Leonie, Mike or Lynaire were very impressed. I was uncomfortable, but I put that down to nervousness at presenting new material. And the participants? Well, I think they were politely silent – a message in itself – out of respect for me.

It was a huge learning experience. I needed to improve my presentation skills and I needed to be very, very familiar with what I was presenting. The area I was entering was not maths or science. It is relatively straightforward to teach geometry, algebra, the laws of thermodynamics or how a plant photosynthesises. These are facts. But the field of human personal development is often very subjective. Stephen Covey is brilliant and he communicates his messages in his own way, but trying to copy him was a mistake. I had to develop my own approach based on – what?

Strategic Planning

The answer came when the Chief Executive of the *Irish Farmers Journal* asked me to head up a team to develop a business plan for the company. Being asked was a huge compliment and, after some consultation, I accepted. I was given a generous operating budget and a huge amount of freedom to access the best available information on business planning. So I started reading widely and talking with business people – and found that I could access one of the best tried-and-tested business planning approaches in Ireland through my contact with the Kerry Group.

In 2008 the Kerry Group was one of the most successful Irish companies and had become a world leader in the area of food ingredients. I had built up good working relationships with top management, especially Denis Brosnan, Hugh Friel and John O'Callaghan, and was able to visit them and to learn how they planned a successful business.

I learnt about leadership, strategic planning, goal-setting, mission statements, and – crucially – the importance of everyone in the company understanding and buying into the strategic planning process. Denis and Hugh believed in company employees taking responsibility for and carrying out all planning processes, without the aid of outside planning consultants. I believe this is essential: not just for a business, but also for the individual as I was proving in my own life.

It is easy for a business to hire in a consultant and ask them to devise a strategic plan. The consultant will do his or her best and will eventually present a very good plan to management. But whose plan is it: the consultant's or the manager's? It's the same as when an individual asks an advisor or consultant, 'What should I do?' These professionals can give an answer, but the answer is often based on what they would do if they were in the other person's shoes. The advice cannot take into account the huge range of information about the client's values, strengths and weaknesses, needs, wants, ambitions, and so on. No wonder that 'The best laid plans go oft astray', to misquote Robbie Burns.

The Kerry Group approach was different. The business plan had to be *their* plan and reflect the values, aspirations, concerns and issues of company owners, management and employees. We took the same approach as we prepared two successive strategic business plans for the *Irish Farmers Journal*. Thankfully, although I'm no longer with the *IFJ*, the plans have been a significant factor in the recent success of the company.

For me personally this was a hugely valuable learning experience. If I was to make presentations on personal development (as we called it at the time) on the Wealth Creation Course, I had to internalise my understanding of it so that I could implement the principles in my own life and help others to do the same. I had to become what I wanted to teach.

Mission statements

One of the key outcomes in the Kerry strategic planning process was the mission statement. In fact this was seen as a 'must have' for any serious business of any size. I tried to incorporate it into the second WCC with mixed success: it seemed like a good idea, because I was trying to extend the principles of business planning into life planning. I had attended a Covey '7 Habits' course and that had also focused on a personal mission statement. The problem was that my understanding of how to construct a statement was very unclear: my early attempts were probably pretty poor. I found that it was relatively easy to transfer the business components of a business statement into a personal statement – but where were the personal components coming from and what, in fact, should they be?

I decided to study the structure of a mission statement more closely and I found that there are three main components: **identity**, **purpose** and **success** measures:

1. A description of the company and the kind of business it is involved with – the company's **identity**.

2. An outline of the company objectives – its **purpose**.

3. Key success indicators. These are ways that allow management and owners to measure the performance of the company – its level of **success**.

The purpose of a business mission statement is to ensure clarity on what the business is all about, define how its success will be measured, and provide a sort of guiding light for management when making business decisions. For example, take a hypothetical company called Alpha Beta Ltd:

☞ Alpha Beta Ltd manufactures snow booties for huskies (**identity**).

☞ Our objective is to profitably lengthen the working lives

of huskies in Alaska and Canada (**purpose**).

🖙 Alpha Beta Ltd aims to achieve a turnover of $500,000 by 2015 and achieve a profit before tax margin of 20 per cent (**success** measures).

Company mission statements typically contain much more information – much of which is often of little use – but these are the three most important factors, since their clear expression keeps management focused and allows owners to judge whether management is doing a good job or poor job.

Successful companies allocate considerable time and resources to developing a clear, authentic mission statement that acts as a beacon for owners, management, employees and customers. This statement will be expanded into a strategic business plan and both the mission statement and the business plan are reviewed and updated regularly – usually annually.

I was given the opportunity to try out these new concepts at a business course run by some friends of mine in the UK in 2001. I devised a series of exercises and questions to help the participants to develop 'identity' and 'success' statements and everyone seemed very happy with the results. Following on from that experience, I decided to introduce the concept of personal mission statements, identity statements and success statements to the next Wealth Creation Course. I found it easier to deal with each separately and come up with a combined product that would help individuals describe what their life was all about and how they could judge the level of success they achieved.

I have used this approach in courses ever since. It has worked well, although I am seriously revisiting the structuring of a personal mission statement (Chapter 16 handles this in more detail).

Human beings are very different from limited companies, but the principles for expressing a company mission statement are, in essence, the same as those that relate to self-knowledge.

And remember that your life is more important to you than any business. What time and resources are you willing to devote to finding a sense of direction and the self-knowledge that will enable you to live a successful and meaningful life? Think of the time you have spent in education and training for your career. Surely developing your personal mission statement and life plan deserve at least the same time and commitment? Will you make that commitment?

During the next three Wealth Creation Courses, Lynaire Ryan, Michael Murphy, Lori Fitzgerald (who replaced Leonie Foster) and I developed a stronger focus on strategic planning, both business and personal. We were constantly learning and developing the content, both for the benefit of participants and ourselves. One of the most important developments was the concept of the **Three Ws** – a structured process for planning. The concept was not new, but the way we presented it made it easy to understand and to use as part of a strategic planning process. (See Chapter 9 for a full explanation.)

Life Coaching, 2005

Needless to say, I had been using the skills and knowledge I was acquiring, not only to make presentations, but also to plan my own life. By 2004, I was clear on a number of issues:

- My mental and physical health was good (although there was one more scare to come).

- My interest in my job as dairy editor of the *IFJ* had declined considerably and I had moved on to write a 'Life and Money' column.

- My personal financial position was good and I would be able to retire reasonably comfortably in four years when I was sixty.

From these conclusions, the main elements of my personal plan took shape: focus on maintaining good health, improving finances and retiring at sixty. But into what lifestyle was I going to retire? It's easy to retire *from* a job. But what did I want to do next? I knew that I wanted to continue working at something that would involve some writing and helping people, but I had no idea what that 'something' might be.

Then came the great breakthrough. I was reading the *Irish Examiner* one day and an ad for a Life and Business Coaching Diploma caught my eye. It was a small ad – only a name and number – but it made me pick up the phone and talk with Ann Boylan, a qualified life coach who leads the course in Cork City. We arranged a meeting and I walked away convinced that this was the career path for me: it fitted my criteria perfectly, since it involved helping people work on themselves and what they wanted in life.

In 2005 I gained a Diploma in Life and Business Coaching. This was a major turning point in my life. Before I began the course in September 2004, my original personal plan was in place. By the time I finished the diploma in April 2005, I had resigned from the *IFJ* to start up a new business and really live the life I had visualised for myself. I became a classic example of positive life coaching in action.

Seven short months, but so much happened during that time. Firstly, life coaching blended in with what I had already discovered to create a full personal development package. Secondly, I saw the amazing results that life coaching can achieve, because I experienced the assistance of a skilled life coach in focusing on my own life.

Life coaching is a relationship between two people, client and coach. Essentially the life coaching process is about helping the client define success and the means of achieving it. The coach's only agenda is to help the client move forward, making the changes and taking the actions to achieve the success he or she desires. During the coaching process the skills of the coach enable the client to define what he or she really wants. Then it is a matter of setting goals and taking action. A very important aspect of coaching is that it addresses the client's whole life, not just the issue or problem they bring up for coaching. I particularly love the Wheel of Life approach (see Chapter 11), which looks at all areas of a client's life and their appropriate balance in that individual's life.

The following quote from the book, *Co-Active Coaching* (Whitworth et al) neatly summarises what coaching is all about: 'The coach's job is to help clients articulate their dreams, desires and aspirations, help them clarify their mission, purpose and goals, and help them achieve that outcome.' That sums it up perfectly and it is the reason I took the Life Coaching Diploma Course.

The course was very interactive. As I mentioned earlier, we were all asked to choose a life coach of our own for the duration of the course – in this way we could experience coaching from the client's perspective. I chose Julie Silfverberg, a life coach who runs Success Partners at Kinsale in County Cork. Julie asked me to bring a real issue to our first session. And boy, did I have a real, live issue!

Career change

While I studied for my diploma, I was still with the *IFJ* in my new capacity as a journalist covering life and money issues. The previous autumn there had been a change of editor in my section – with an accompanying change in editorial policy, not to mention a personality clash between the new editor and various staff members, including myself. So when I arrived for my three coaching sessions with Julie I brought with me a live, burning issue: I was deeply unhappy with my work, but still imagined myself sticking it out until sixty before retiring. There were three years to go and I was counting. So, when I turned up to be coached by Julie, I did not have to concoct an issue to be coached on – I had a serious problem.

At the first session I wanted to talk about the problem but, curiously, Julie kept steering me away from it and getting me to look at it from different perspectives. Then during the second session, when I tried again to focus on the problem, she asked a simple question that stopped me in my tracks: 'So, Con, what is your ideal outcome from the current situation?' I replied that I did not think my ideal outcome was possible. She asked me to describe it anyway – assuming everything was possible – and, as my homework, to write it down in my learning journal. While writing this chapter, I have opened that old journal so I can relay my words to you, just as I wrote them on 28 February 2005:

My ideal outcome is:

- retire from the *IFJ*;

- negotiate a severance package worth €X;

- negotiate a two-year contract as a freelance writer to bring in €Y per annum;

- develop a life-coaching business.

Things happened very fast after that. The following day – yes, the first day of March 2005 – I was speaking to the financial controller at the *IFJ* and discovered that a severance package was a possibility, something I had believed was impossible. This changed everything. Now, instead of focusing on the problem, I was focusing on a wonderful solution. I discussed the situation with two friends and my wife, Eleanor, and worked out the figures. Then, on 24 March, I reached an agreement that gave me everything, and more, that I had described in my ideal outcome just twenty-five days previously! Was that not the clearest possible demonstration of life coaching in action? It was truly amazing – I know that you may say there were things outside my control that helped me secure my goal and that I was lucky. Or perhaps it was a coincidence that company policy on severance packages had changed. I'll go into what happens when you set clear goals in Chapter 11, but for now here's a story and a quote that may help explain the apparently unexplainable. W. H. Murray wrote about his experiences in *The Scottish Himalayan Expedition*, 1951:

> We had definitely committed ourselves . . . and we had put down our passage money and booked a sailing to Bombay. This may sound too simple, but is great in consequence. Until one is committed, there is hesitancy, the chance to draw back, always ineffectiveness. Concerning all acts of initiative (and creation), there is one elementary truth the ignorance of which kills countless ideas and splendid plans . . .

And then Murray wrote those famous words, so often mistakenly attributed to Goethe:

> the moment one definitely commits oneself, then Providence moves too . . . A whole series of events issues from the decision, raising in one's favour all manner of unforeseen incidents, meetings and material assistance, which no man could have dreamt would have come his way.

I committed myself in March 2005: I negotiated a satisfactory severance package with the *IFJ* and indeed 'Providence moved too' and 'unforeseen incidents and meetings' did render 'material assistance'. With the result that, on the last day of June, I departed from the *IFJ* in great spirits to: a) take a two-month holiday; and b) begin a new self-employed career in September. As good an example as you will get of life coaching in action!

And I spent that precious two-month 'holiday' at home. Strange you may say, but perhaps not so strange when I tell you that we live on the coast near a beautiful village in West Cork. It has it all – sea, sandy beach, fishing, swimming, warm, friendly people and a great social life in the village, which boasts four pubs and good food. Our home was only three years old, so there was plenty for me to do developing the garden. It was my longest 'holiday' ever – and in a very beautiful part of the world.

I qualified as a life coach in April 2005 and then September came – and with it self-employment. I was excited and a little apprehensive as well. The reality was that I was leaving a secure job that delivered a very healthy salary cheque every month. I had exchanged this for a small pension that, with the writing contract I had negotiated at the same time as my severance package from *IFJ*, would leave us about €30,000 short to cover our annual living costs after paying income tax. Initially, I assumed that most of this would come from life coaching. I started with six clients and charged €100 per hour. This was in the upper range of fees, but I felt comfortable charging it because I knew that I would deliver excellent value to my clients. And, to date, the clients I have coached have benefited enormously. I set out to work with people who wanted to achieve personal and financial success in their lives. I tell my clients that I will help them to define what personal and financial success means for *them* – everyone has a different definition of success. Then I help them set goals; finally I encourage and motivate them to take the necessary steps and actions to move towards their personal and financial goals.

Despite my enthusiasm for life coaching, it became obvious very quickly that earning €30,000 a year coaching individual clients was unrealistic. Life coaching was new in Ireland and the demand simply was not there, especially outside Dublin, the main population centre. Then, just to show yet again that 'unforeseen incidents' render 'material assistance', a number of rural organisations requested that I present one- and two-day courses to small groups of fifteen to twenty people. Over the past four years these have provided a valuable stream of income. One course focuses on Personal Life Planning and the other on Personal Financial Planning. On top of that came a demand for more Wealth Creation Courses. So Lori, Lynaire, Michael and I presented another WCC in the autumn of 2005, followed by two more in 2007 and 2008. Income problems almost solved.

To date, I am delighted with my new career, which involves some personal life coaching, presenting training courses and writing. I get a great sense of satisfaction and joy when I see a person confidently taking control of their lives. I'm happy knowing that I have helped people to help themselves – that's what my coaching, training and writing is all about.

I remember being asked at a meeting once what I saw as the central purpose of my life. I answered, 'I want to leave the world a better place for my descendents and all others on the planet.' I remember thinking that this sounded very grandiose, but I realised that this goal plays a major role in giving my life purpose and meaning. Involvement in coaching, training and writing help me to know that I am making a valuable contribution to the world – and that is why I'm writing this book. What's more, coaching and training have given me the practical experience and certainty that the processes I'll describe in the following chapters really work.

CHAPTER 4

YOUR PERSONAL LEARNING JOURNAL

THIS BOOK WILL CHANGE YOUR LIFE!

How often have you read that in the advertising blurb in a book review or on a book cover? The truth, of course, is that no book in itself can change your life. It's what you do as a result of reading the book that changes your life. I hope that in reading this book you will make changes to enhance the quality of your life.

However, I want to introduce you a book that really *will* change your life: your Personal Learning Journal. This is a book that I hope you will begin as you work through the remaining chapters of *Yes I Can* – and one that I strongly encourage you to continue through the rest of your life. I started my first Personal Learning Journal in 2000, and the first entry was on 4 September, while I was walking the Dingle Way in County Kerry. I am now on my tenth Journal and I know I'll be filling pages and books for the rest of my life.

The idea for a Personal Learning Journal (let's call it a PLJ) came from a man called Barry McCullough, who contributed to our second Wealth Creation Course and a few small courses that Eleanor and I ran. Barry tackled the process of goal-setting and taking control of your life with missionary zeal, and it was his suggestion that a strong motivator might be a PLJ.

The PLJ is not a diary and you do not have to write in it every day. I write in mine whenever I feel the need. I see my journal as a way of talking with myself about issues that are important to me. I write about what's happening in my life at the moment, how I'm reacting to things mentally. I use the PLJ to make plans, set goals and record the results. I use it to measure how I'm progressing in life, especially in relation to my happiness and satisfaction with life.

Overall, my PLJs are about *me*. They record my journey of self-discovery as I live new experiences and think new thoughts – although it took me a few years to realise that this journey was my true focus. Sometimes these experiences are dramatic, as when I moved on from the *Irish Farmers Journal*. Then there are smaller experiences like planning a summer barbeque, a night out with friends, or the things I have learnt from a book or article I have just read. Thoughts and ideas come from everywhere – books, conversations, visits and holidays – and sometimes just out of the blue. I often have night-time brainstorms and I may get up at 3.00 a.m. to record my thoughts in my journal. For me, they are fascinating to read, but they are not for anyone else. I regard them as extremely private and Eleanor and my children respect that privacy. It took a few years for me to realise that my PLJs are a record of my voyage of self-discovery. They record *how* I learn and *what* I am learning about myself.

I'm telling you about my own journal at this point in the book because I think you'll find that this is a perfect time to start your own. Buy a hardcover book with lined pages – A5 or slightly larger is a good size. I suggest you buy a good quality book. After all, it's your life story and it will be around for a long time. Then just start writing: you will find plenty to write about as you progress through the rest of *Yes I Can*. Over time you will build up a wonderful record and reference of your life and the progress you are making.

By now you know that the seed for this book was born of my experiences following the diagnosis with depression in 1996 – but you may well wonder what my family background is and what I did for the first forty-eight years of my life. That's a book in itself, but I will give you a brief synopsis.

Both my parents came from small, mountainy farms inland from Bantry, West Cork. They left to find work in London, met and married, then returned to Ireland to have their family: I was the first, born in 1948, and three more brothers and a sister followed. I lived in four different places in the first six years of my life before my parents moved the family back to England – to Dagenham, where my father found work, like many Irish, in the massive Henry Ford factory.

Living in London was a formative experience, and it was only much later that I realised what had I learnt about myself while I was there. For example, I found that I got great satisfaction helping people – it's no surprise, therefore, that writing to help farm families for thirty years and working as a life coach have given me so much fulfilment.

I also learnt that I did not want to spend my life living in a city. I loved geography at school and countries with wide-open spaces greatly appealed to me – the USA, Australia and especially Canada. By the time I was thirteen, I was an expert on Canada and had actually applied for a work visa. The Canadian government wrote back telling me that I was the youngest applicant they had ever entertained and kindly advised me to continue my education and apply again when I was eighteen. Perhaps this letter influenced my parents, because they made a decision to return to Ireland in 1962.

They farmed for a while and then bought a big pub in Cork City. I was back to the city again and I lived there on and off for some eighteen more years. But there are cities and cities – Cork is a village in comparison to London. I greatly enjoyed school, university and sport in Cork, and I married a Cork girl, Eleanor O'Keeffe. But I still longed for the country. For me rural life represents open spaces, warm, friendly people and a sense of community, of belonging – I was unable to satisfy my needs for these things in a city.

I mention the word 'needs', and I will come back to this in Chapter 15. However, when I was younger I did not associate the concept of having 'needs' with my own feeling that something was missing: I just knew that I wanted to live and work in the countryside. My first attempt was to buy a large farm in West Cork. For a variety of reasons, this venture did not work and I (we) lost nearly everything in 1983. I was facing bankruptcy and, if it had not been for the superb support of Eleanor, I might have taken my own life. She was the one who inspired me to realise what was really important in life: namely our marriage and our three children. Property and money were insignificant in comparison. This was a major, major learning experience and it has (mostly) stayed with me ever since. I say mostly, because I lost focus again a decade later and ended up with Dr X, which is where we came in at the start of *Yes I Can*.

So that's me. Why is it important? Well, in effect, a life history is an introduction to the rationale behind a person's current values and goals – and 'needs'– and these are crucial to life planning. Now we'll move on to Parts Two and Three – the place where it all begins to happen for *you*. The place where I hope you will find all the skills and tools to help you create the life you want and to ensure that you bring happiness, meaning and success into that life.

First I want to fire you up a bit, so that you are eager to learn these skills and tools. After all, it will take a bit of work, commitment and time to start planning your life. Why would you bother? Try this exercise – the first one for your Personal Learning Journal. I hope it will make you sit up and say, 'Hey, let's get onto Parts Two and Three without delay.'

SELF-ASSESSMENT PROCESS 1:

YOUR LIFETIME CHART

The chart below is based on an average lifespan of eighty years, which is how long a man or woman lives in the western world, and the first chart is mine.

Con's Life Time Chart									
1	2	3	4	5	6	7	8	9	10
11	12	13	14	15	16	17	18	19	20
21	22	23	24	25	26	27	28	29	30
31	32	33	34	35	36	37	38	39	40
41	42	43	44	45	46	47	48	49	50
51	52	53	54	55	56	57	58	59	60
61	62	63	64	65	66	67	68	69	70
71	72	73	74	75	76	77	78	79	80

Figure 1: Con's LifeTime Chart.

The next chart is for you.

My Life Time Chart									
1	2	3	4	5	6	7	8	9	10
11	12	13	14	15	16	17	18	19	20
21	22	23	24	25	26	27	28	29	30
31	32	33	34	35	36	37	38	39	40
41	42	43	44	45	46	47	48	49	50
51	52	53	54	55	56	57	58	59	60
61	62	63	64	65	66	67	68	69	70
71	72	73	74	75	76	77	78	79	80

Figure 2: Empty LifeTime Chart for the reader to fill in

- I suggest you copy the blank chart and paste it into your PLJ.

- Then fill in the squares for the years that you have lived so far. A surprising first page in your journal?

- What is this exercise telling you? Write down your thoughts.

I know what this exercise said to me. It said, 'Con, you've twenty years left on the clock. Better make the best possible use of them. Another square will be gone next year. What are *you* going to do with the rest of *your* life?' How will you answer that question – what are you going to do with the rest of your life?

PART TWO:

TAKING CONTROL

CHAPTER 5: WHO IS RESPONSIBLE FOR MY LIFE?

(PLJ Exercise Self-Assessment Process 2: Where am I now and how did I get here?;

PLJ Exercise Self-Assessment Process 3: Where am I going?)

Choices, Decisions and Actions Determine my Future

CHAPTER 6: FIVE CHOICES FOR EVERY SITUATION

A World of No Choice

The Five Choices

Accept the status quo; Change something about the situation; Change your attitude; Get out!; Plan strategically (PLJ Exercise Self-assessment Process 4: Choices).

CHAPTER 7: EXPANDING YOUR CHOICES AND OPTIONS

Strategies to Increase Your Options
Brainstorming; Modelling; Lateral Thinking (PLJ Exercise Self-Assessment Process 5: Broadening your options).

CHAPTER 8: ATTITUDE DETERMINES YOUR LIFE

What is Attitude?

How to Foster an Empowering Attitude
Five choices; Beliefs; Think positively; Choose your information; Focus on the best; Think before responding; Choose your associates; Ask empowering questions; There is no such thing as failure, only results.

The Six Characteristics of a Positive Attitude
Inner motivation; High standards; Taking small steps towards a goal; Focusing on the present, with an eye to the future; Personal involvement; Self-to-self comparison.

The Glass is Always Half-full

CHAPTER 5

WHO IS RESPONSIBLE FOR MY LIFE?

I BELIEVE THAT WE ARE ALL MASTER OF OUR OWN DESTINY.
WE ARE WHO WE ARE BECAUSE WE MADE A CHOICE TO BE
WHO WE ARE. PEOPLE MUST TAKE RESPONSIBILITY FOR
THEMSELVES; THEY CANNOT BLAME PARENTS OR OTHERS.
REMEMBER THAT YOU ALWAYS HAVE THE CHOICE TO BE
DIFFERENT.

JIM VAN DER POEL, NEW ZEALAND FARMER

'Who is responsible for my life?' is a serious and fundamental question. Your answer will have a huge influence on how the rest of your life takes shape.

SELF-ASSESSMENT PROCESS 2:

WHERE AM I NOW AND HOW DID I GET HERE?

Look at your present reality first, since this reflects much of what has happened in your past. Now try to answer the following questions as objectively as possible:

What relationships do you have?

How is your health?

What career or job do you have?

What is your financial position?

Where do you live?

Take as much time as you need and also think about any other areas of your life that are important to you. Write the answers down. As I will explain later, writing things down is far, far better than just running ideas and thoughts through your head. Now that you have a fairly thorough, written description of your current life situation, here comes the big question:

What has caused or determined who and where I am today? Put differently, the question is: who or what is responsible for my current life situation? Write down your thoughts and answers.

Great discussion ensues when I put the second question to groups on my courses. Using a flipchart we are able to break the key influences into three sections:

my **genes** (inherited characteristics);

the **environment** I have grown up and lived in (my conditioning); and

my **behaviour** or the choices, decisions and actions I have taken.

People learn a lot about themselves when they consider how important each factor has been as a contributor to their current life situation. A few people believe that their genes are mostly responsible for where they are today. The majority believe that it is their conditioning and environment – the circumstances of their childhood and early adulthood – that are the biggest factors. They point to the family situations they grew up in, the location they lived in, their friends, teachers and employers, the society and culture they live in, politics, religion, the media, and so on. Then there are a few people who believe that their own choices, decisions and actions are the factors that have mainly determined their current life situation.

Who is right? Actually, they are all right to some extent. And we could spend hours debating which factor is the most important. The really important question comes next.

SELF-ASSESSMENT PROCESS 3:

WHERE AM I GOING?

What will cause or determine who and where I will be in future? Who or what is responsible for my future life situation?

- Think of what you would like your life situation to be in five years, in five months, in five weeks, in five days – or even just in five minutes. Think carefully and make a note of your thoughts.

- Who or what determines what role you will play or how you will behave in these situations? Write down your thoughts and answers.

What will be the most important factors as you move into the future? Will it be your genes? Sure, they have determined the colour of your eyes and the shape of your body. But at this stage they have little or no influence on your future. Will it be your conditioning that determines your future? Yes, it can do – if you allow it, if you choose it. It's a choice. A person can continue to say, 'Well I left school at sixteen, so I won't be able to become a manager.' Or, 'I lost all my money ten years ago, so I'll never be wealthy.' You can choose to allow the circumstances of your past life determine to your future – this is *your* choice. The third alternative is the one that empowers people.

Choices, Decisions and Actions Determine my Future

You are in control of your life. Yes there will be some limits. For example, if you are 5 feet tall, your chances of becoming a professional basketball player are about nil. The same applies if you have an accident and are confined to a wheelchair. A gold medal in the high jump becomes out of the question. At this stage, I hear you protesting loudly and pointing out all the opportunities there are for vertically challenged and handicapped people. Of course there are – provided they *choose* these opportunities and decide to take control over their futures, whatever the limitations they face. In fact, the marvellous achievements of people handicapped by all sorts of issues clearly demonstrate the power of the third determining factor in making us who we are. The truth is that, irrespective of your genetics and conditioning, you can choose to make the decisions and take the actions that will determine your future.

I find that once they think this through, most people on my courses and all my private clients choose to take control of their futures. It is such an important step and attitude that I stay with it as long as it takes for them to believe in it – and themselves.

At this point in a group discussion, I find that someone always asks, 'Hold on a minute, what about outside, unforeseen circumstances? There can be accidents, stock market crashes, rising oil prices, company closures, floods and famine. These are going to affect my future – and I have no control over them.'

So let's consider those outside circumstances over which

you have no control, still focusing on what you *always* have control over – your reaction in the moment. Perhaps the company you work for closes down and you lose your job. What have you got control over? Your attitude and your response. It is just as Jawaharlal Nehru, first Prime Minister of India said, 'Life is like a game of cards. The hand that is dealt you is determinism, the way you play it is free will.' It is definitely up to us how we play our hand.

The life of Victor Frankl, an Austrian Jewish psychiatrist who spent the Second World War incarcerated in the Nazi concentration camps at Auschwitz and Dachau, was a most remarkable illustration of this principle. That was some 'hand of cards' he was dealt: extreme life circumstances and exceptionally challenging conditions, in which everything could be taken from a person – possessions, clothes, food, relations, and often life itself. Everything? No, not everything. For his insight under these appalling conditions was Frankl's great contribution to human psychology and philosophy – and indeed life coaching, although such a thing did not exist in Frankl's time. He questioned the belief that a human being is completely and unavoidably influenced and controlled by outside circumstances – in his case the awful concentration camp surroundings – and he asked:

> But what about human liberty? Is there no spiritual freedom in regard to behaviour and reaction to any given surroundings? Is that theory true, which would have us believe that man is no more than a product of many conditional and environmental factors – be they of a biological, psychological or sociological nature? Is man but an accidental product of these?
>
> The experiences of camp life show that man does have a choice of action. Man *can* preserve a vestige of spiritual freedom, of independence of mind, even in such terrible

conditions of psychic and physical stress. We, who lived in concentration camps, can remember the men who walked through the huts comforting others, giving away their last piece of bread. They may have been few in number, but they offer sufficient proof that *everything can be taken from a man but one thing: the last of the human freedoms — to choose one's attitude* [response] *in any given set of circumstances, to choose one's own way* [my italics].

(*Man's Search for Meaning*, 1946)

I find this belief, this statement, mind-blowing in its implications for life planning. Viktor Frankl, in terrible circumstances, chose to take 100 per cent responsibility for his response and attitude. He found that when a person takes responsibility and finds meaning in his life, he can have peace of mind under any conditions. I believe the same is true for every person who wants to live a happy, fulfilled life, irrespective of the circumstances they encounter. Make a decision to take 100 per cent responsibility for your future, whatever circumstances life may throw at you.

So now we come to the final question in this chapter: 'Do I take 100 per cent responsibility for making the choices and decisions or taking the actions that will determine my future?' Still not sure? Maybe you only feel like taking 80 per cent or 90 per cent responsibility? Sorry, but that is not really good enough, is it? Think about it – is responsibility for the other 10 to 20 per cent of circumstances really beyond your control? Of course, there is a benefit to be had from giving responsibility away to factors outside your control. You will have something or someone to blame if things go wrong – and you will always be able to find plenty of excuses, such as:

☞ The stock market crashed so I lost all my money.

☞ I didn't hit my sales targets because my secretary was sick.

My marriage broke up because my wife didn't love me any more.

Great excuses, but think of what these people would have said if they were totally committed to and responsible for making money, reaching sales targets and cultivating a happy marriage.

What will your answer be? Will you choose to be entirely responsible for your future? 'Yes, I take 100 per cent responsibility for my future.' Write it down in your PLJ. How do you feel after making that bold statement? People find it both frightening and inspiring when they decide (choose) to take responsibility for their futures.

We can now move on to the next key question: 'How do we make the right decisions and take the right actions to ensure we live the life that we want to live?' The next chapter will look at the vital role of choices in the Life Planning Process.

CHAPTER 6

FIVE CHOICES FOR EVERY SITUATION

IN THE LONG RUN WE SHAPE OUR LIVES AND WE SHAPE
OURSELVES. THE PROCESS NEVER ENDS UNTIL WE DIE. AND
THE CHOICES WE MAKE ARE ULTIMATELY OUR OWN RESPONSI-
BILITY.

(ELEANOR ROOSEVELT)

A World of No Choice

Your life is lived through the choices, decisions and actions you take every moment of the day. However, many people trap themselves in a world of no choice. You will recognise this in the language they use:

☞ I've *got to* mow the lawn today.

☞ I *have to* go to work tomorrow.

☞ I've *only got* three weeks' holidays.

By habitually using these words and language patterns, people become prisoners of the 'one-choice' syndrome and they give away control of their lives to things outside themselves – the lawn, work, working conditions. Paradoxically, they are still making a choice, although it is done unconsciously. This is also a form of mental laziness. Sometimes, it's easier to be the victim and prisoner of circumstances rather than to do a bit of thinking and planning and develop other choices and options. This self-victimisation and laziness becomes apparent in the words they use:

- No, I can't take you to the beach because I've *got to* mow the lawn today.

- Sunday is a bit of a bummer, because I *have to* go to work tomorrow.

- I've an awful job but I *must* stick at it because I need the money.

- I'd really love to visit you, but I've *only got* three weeks' holidays.

The paradox of these statements is that the people who make them recognise that, yes, there are other important things in life, but they cannot do them because they 'have got to' or 'have to' or 'must do' or 'only have' something else. People get stuck in this line of thought and many of them lead miserable, negative lives as a result.

The Five Choices

The reality can be very different because I know that there are *always* at least five choices in every life situation:

1. **Accept** the status quo.

2. **Change something** about the situation, if possible.

3. **Change your attitude** to the situation.

4. **Get out** – move on to something else.

5. **Plan** strategically.

Accept the status quo

There are two variations on this, one healthy and one unhealthy. Firstly, if you are satisfied with the situation you are in, it may well be a good choice to stick with it. After all, as they say, 'If it ain't broke, don't fix it'. However sometimes, although you may be satisfied with where you are, there may be better options available. So it is always worthwhile seeking and considering other choices. We will come to that later.

Secondly, you may be unhappy and dissatisfied with the situation you are in, but you choose to accept it and stick with it. You do not like it – but you 'must' stick with it, because you 'can't' do something else, or you 'have to . . .' do another thing. And so it goes on – all of the 'prisoner' expressions are dragged into use. Your life is like a 10-foot square cell and you are stuck there – for life. This is very unhealthy. Your language shows that you clearly do not like it and you moan, groan and complain. People in this mode become bitter and angry and suffer from anxiety and stress. But let's be clear, it *is* a choice and you should recognise this, for it is the choice *you* are making.

These people are not fun to be with. In fact they are downright negative and this negativity will rub off on you if you let it. Think about some of the complainers and moaners you know. You meet them in the pub, the supermarket, at work, after church. Do not let their negativity rub off on you. So if you think you might be in the 'one-choice prisoner mode', move swiftly on, because this is not *really* you, is it?

Change something about the situation

Let's imagine that you are in a situation you do not like. However, for whatever reason, you choose to stay in it. It could be a job, a relationship, almost anything. Ask yourself this question: 'What can *I* do to change this situation to make it better for me?' By asking what 'I' can do, you are taking control and this is very empowering. You move away from being a victim or prisoner of the situation to taking charge.

For example, I coached a person who was very unhappy in his job and he was thinking of leaving – we'll call him Michael. Michael's function was to provide information for company projects. He was good at his job as a researcher but felt bored and frustrated as a 'back-room' worker. A co-worker from a different department, which Michael thought of as more exciting and closer to the cutting edge, would make a request for information that was needed. Michael carried out the research and gave the report to the project leader and then moved on to the next research request. During coaching, I asked Michael to think about what he could change to remove the boredom and frustration. He discovered that he would love to know what happened to the project and how his research was used. So he changed his working relationship with the project teams. He formed a link that allowed him to see how the project progressed and talk with the people carrying out the project. He could then see how his research was used. This simple change gave much more meaning to his work and more connection with colleagues. The result is that he has remained in the same job – but in a much happier frame of mind.

But what can you do if you are unable to change the situation?

Change your attitude

This is easy to illustrate with the story about the tourist passing a building site on a cold winter's day. Two men were building a wall with concrete blocks. The tourist was curious to know what was being built. 'Good day,' he said to the first man, 'What are you building?' 'Good day my butt,' the man replied with a slight sneer, 'What's good about it? It's cold and my hands are freezing and I'm fed up mixing mortar and laying block after block making a wall for some sort of council building.' Ouch!

The tourist moved on a few metres to the other man and asked the same question. 'Good day, and what are you building?' 'Oh hello,' the second man replied with a smile, 'This is part of a wall for the new city library that some day will be full of wonderful books for me and other citizens to read. I really like biographies so I'm looking forward to finishing the wall and joining the library.'

Same cold day, same mortar, same blocks, same wall, same trade – but two totally different attitudes. I would suggest that if you find yourself in a situation that you do not much like, but in which you still *choose* to remain, it might be worth asking yourself these questions:

- What aspects of this situation do I like?

- What's good about this situation?

- Is the purpose of what I am doing something that I can feel good about?

Keep looking for something positive and meaningful and then identify with it.

Recently, I came across a very good example of attitude change with my brother-in-law, John, who is a missionary priest in Nigeria. He was ministering in a town with a mixture of Christians and Muslims, who generally get on well together. Five times each day, the muezzin calls the Muslim flock to prayer from the minaret at the top of the mosque. Problems arose when a high-volume loudspeaker system was installed. This upset the Christians – not just for religious reasons, but also because of the disturbance to sleep and normal life. Father John was annoyed and upset at first. Then he considered his options and decided to change his attitude. 'The muezzin calls people to prayer, and, since I am also a man of prayer, I will pray too.'

This story emphasises that in all situations it makes sense to consider the options open to you, just like the blocklayer and the priest did. You may find that a simple shift in attitude works wonders. But what can you do if, having tried to change the situation and your attitude, you still do not like the situation you are in?

Get out

The world is full of prisoners. Their prison walls are the businesses they own, the locations they live in, the relationships they are in and the work they do. These people are mostly prisoners by choice, even though they may not realise it. And they have the key to freedom in their hands. It's labelled, 'Get out!' or 'Move on!'

I have done a lot of work with farmers and self-employed professionals who are unhappy in life. They feel tied to their careers, usually because they have inherited the farm or a parent has been in same profession (medicine, law, accountancy, and so on). These clients became farmers, doctors, lawyers and accountants by default. Looking back to their teens, they may see that they succumbed to parental pressure. The choices they made seemed right at the time because they were made in order to keep other people happy – and that made them feel happy for a time. But finally they woke up one morning and found that they hated what they were doing.

Many of these people soldiered on, bound by the walls and chains of parental expectations. But others rebelled and got out. My brother Michael inherited the family farm. For a number of years he was very enthusiastic and an excellent farmer. However, he realised he was not really happy farming, and, with my father's blessing, he sold up and bought a block of apartments in the city. He's much happier – and wealthier – and is now in a loving relationship. He chose to move on instead of choosing to remain in a situation he did not like.

So, if you find yourself in any of the following problem situations, realise that you also have the choice to 'get out'. There is one major danger with the 'get out' choice. You can end up in a worse situation than the one you left – we all know about 'out of the frying pan into the fire'. That situation is quite common when a person builds up a lot of pressure and stress in the problem situation. Then, in a snap decision, a knee-jerk reaction, they get out and end up worse off than before.

Marrying someone on the 'rebound' is a classic example. A person storms out of an unhappy relationship, falls 'in love' with someone else very quickly, only to find this relationship is worse than the one they left. Another common example is when people retire and sell their homes to live in the sun or some such dream environment. It is estimated that over 50 per cent of people who do this sell up again and move back to where they were originally.

Similar consequences often ensue when people move away from a job, career or business they do not like. The key words here are 'away from'. The person is so preoccupied with what they *do not* like and *do not* want that they fail to 'move towards'

Problem Situation	'Get Out' Response	Next Question?
I don't like the business I own.	Sell up	What business will I go into now?
I don't like where I'm living.	Move house	Where will I move to?
I'm unhappy in this relationship	Separate	Who will I develop a relationship with?
I don't like my work.	Quit	What job will you do now?

Table 1

what they *do* want. Like the person running blindly away from the bull – and over a cliff! Which brings us to the final, and usually best, choice – to choose proactively.

Plan strategically
This choice hinges on one simple but all-powerful question: 'What do I *want*?'

All the other choices we have looked at focus on what a person *does not* want – in other words they are 'away from' choices. Strategic planning is about finding answers to the question, 'What *do* I want?' And then finding ways of turning the answer into a reality. We will come back to this empowering 'towards' choice in Chapters 9, 10 and 11.

SELF-ASSESSMENT PROCESS 4:

CHOICES

- Look back over your life at situations where you felt trapped and restricted in the options open to you. Using the Five Choice approach, what other choices were open to you? This is a learning exercise and not something to feel guilty about. Remember mistakes are really learning experiences.

- Examine some of your current situations and brainstorm the options you may have.

- Practice using the above approach when you are making decisions and use it to help others in work and family situations.

CHAPTER 7

EXPANDING YOUR CHOICES AND OPTIONS

IT IS OUR CHOICES THAT SHOW WHAT WE TRULY ARE, FAR
MORE THAN OUR ABILITIES.

(J. K. ROWLING)

Life is full of opportunities or choices. The challenge is to examine the choices open to us and to choose the ones that are best for us. For this process to work we need to be aware of all of the opportunities and choices available to us. As was mentioned in Chapter 6, many people get stuck in the 'one-choice syndrome'. But we have seen that there are always at least five ways of approaching choice. The truth is that this is not really the end of our options, since in reality we can expand our range of choice even further. (I am using the words 'options' and 'choices' interchangeably.)

But how many options should you have?

📖 **One option** is virtually a command. You are a captive of that option. So it makes good sense to have more than one.

📖 **Two options** are better, except that this can create a dilemma: which one will I select, heads or tails? Two choices lead can lead to anxiety.

☞**Three or more options** are far better. This gives richness of choice and helps a person make better decisions.

Strategies to Increase Your Options

What is the best way to go about discovering and creating more options in your life?

Brainstorming

The purpose of this process is to identify as many options as possible. The purpose is *not* to analyse or judge each option. Just get the suggestions down. So, if you are doing it yourself, just get every option that comes into your head down on paper. Evaluation of the options comes later.

You will usually get more options from brainstorming if you get help from other people. Sit a few people down and tell them what you are trying to achieve. Keep your own options to yourself. Then ask them for the options and choices they see as appropriate. Note their suggestions in a notebook or on a flipchart. Again, it is important *not* to allow any discussion on the merits or demerits of different proposals. People love to get into that, but it hinders the creative process. There is another undesirable effect in a group brainstorming session. Shy people may keep their heads down and be slow to make suggestions. If, when they suggest an option, it is blown out of the water by the more vocal members of the group, the shy person will keep his or her head down forever – and of course their potentially gem-like contributions will remain hidden as well.

So, the rules of brainstorming are simple. The objective is to get ideas, options and choices onto paper. It does not matter how 'off-the-wall' an idea may seem, get it down. The selection process will identify which option or choice is most suitable.

Think of the brainstorming session as a way of spreading seeds (ideas) on the soil. The good ones will take root and grow. The unsuitable ones will either not take root at all, or will wither and die soon after germination. At this stage you cannot tell the viable seeds from the unviable ones. Let the evaluation process do that.

Modelling

No, this is not about dressing up and flaunting yourself on a catwalk. It's about finding someone who has been in a situation similar to the one you are facing and finding out what choices they made. If someone has already invented the wheel, why re-invent it yourself? This was the approach I adopted when I was working on the strategic business plan for the *Irish Farmers Journal*. I found a model that worked – that of the Kerry Group – and learnt from their experience. I did not need a degree in business or an MBA, just a clear idea of what we wanted and a successful model to follow. And it worked.

It is often as important to identify failed models. As German chancellor Otto von Bismarck said over a century ago, 'Fools say they learn by experience. I prefer to profit by others' experience.' So if someone has failed in an attempt to do what you want to do, learn from their mistakes so that you can avoid them.

Lateral thinking

This is a technique or process that you can use on your own or, even more effectively, with the help of others. Lateral thinking can be a fun process that really opens up the options and choices available to you. I have learnt three levels of lateral thinking – moving across, moving down and moving up.

1. **Moving across** means looking for alternative ideas, options and choices. The questions to ask are:

☞What other examples are there of this?

☞What other ways are there of achieving this?

2. **Moving up** means thinking of the purpose of the option you are examining. The moving up level is where you look for ideas or options that may be very different but serve the same purpose as the original idea. You might ask a variety of questions about a specific option (remember that the language of the question itself is important, since a slight variation in the tone of a question can elicit a different response):

   ☞For what purpose (why) am I choosing this?

   ☞What is my intention?

   ☞What is this an example of?

   ☞What does this do for me?

3. **Moving down** means looking for specific information on an idea or option. The questions to ask are:

   ☞What *specifically* is this option all about? Explain what the option involves.

   ☞When will I need it?

   ☞When will it happen?

   ☞Where will it take place?

   ☞How can I make it happen or work?

Here are two examples of lateral thinking in action:

EXAMPLE 1: SHEILA WANTS TO BUY A CITROEN CAR. This is a 'one-choice syndrome' situation. Let's improve it:

   ☞**Moving across** question: What are other makes of car

are there? She can come up with a long list: Mercedes, Porsche, Volvo, Renault, Peugeot, Ford, Nissan, Toyota, and so on, to increase her options.

Moving down question: What specifically do I want in a car? Sheila can then look at other factors in order to make a choice. These factors could include price, fuel economy, size and colour. With a more specific description she can move up again and ask, 'What sort of car fits this description?' She may end up with a two-door, 1300cc, red Toyota.

Moving up question: But why do I want a car? She may answer, 'I need a car to get to work every day.'

We have now moved 'up' from wanting a car to the real purpose for the car – Sheila needs transport to get to work. But 'transport' is a big picture, an abstract idea. We need to turn it into specific ideas and options, so the questioning process goes on:

Moving down question: What other specific types of transport could get Sheila to work? She might answer: walking, taking a bus, getting a bicycle, taking a taxi, and travelling with a workmate who lives nearby.

With lateral thinking, the ideas roll out at different levels and provide a rich vein of options and choices.

EXAMPLE 2: I NEED COAL FOR THE FIRE.

Moving across question: 'What else can I use instead of coal?' Some answers may be peat briquettes, logs, waste timber, paper, old clothes – anything that will burn in a fire.

☞**Moving up** question: 'What do you want the fire for?' This asks for purpose, which may be 'to keep warm'. Now that you know the purpose of the fire, you can revert to a

☞**Moving across** question: 'What other ways can I think of to keep warm?' Answers can include covering up with a blanket, insulating the house, wearing warm clothes, installing solar heating or cuddling up with your partner.

Once we have a number of options, the next task is to choose one – in other words, to make a decision – and then follow it up with action. That's just what the rest of Part Two is about.

SELF-ASSESSMENT 5:

BROADENING YOUR OPTIONS

Write down a number of decisions you are about to make and practice uncovering some of the options available to you, using:

☞ brainstorming

☞ modelling

☞ lateral thinking

You should find that you have broadened your choice considerably by the time you have completed the exercise.

CHAPTER 8

ATTITUDE DETERMINES YOUR LIFE

NOTHING CAN STOP THE MAN WITH THE RIGHT MENTAL
ATTITUDE FROM ACHIEVING HIS GOAL; NOTHING ON EARTH
CAN HELP THE MAN WITH THE WRONG MENTAL ATTITUDE.

(THOMAS JEFFERSON)

In my opinion, attitude is a major, if not *the* major, force that
determines our happiness and the quality of our lives. Your
attitude determines what you believe in and your beliefs
determine the circumstances of your life, including how you
live your life – your chosen lifestyle. These, in turn, result in a
quality of life that affects your various human needs and,
ultimately, your happiness.

My conclusion, therefore, is that attitude is of paramount
importance in helping us achieve our goals in life, fulfilling
our needs and enabling us to lead happy, fulfilled and
meaningful lives. The importance of attitude is reflected in the
multitude of quotations about it. American writer James Lane
Allen thought that 'Man's rise or fall, success or failure,
happiness or unhappiness depends on his attitude', and the
philosopher William James said, 'The greatest discovery of my
generation is that man can alter his life simply by altering his
attitude of mind'.

But what exactly *is* attitude and what can you do to develop an 'empowering' attitude – sometimes called a 'positive mental attitude'?

What is Attitude?

In the Oxford English Dictionary, attitude is defined as:

i. a settled opinion or a settled way of thinking;

ii. behaviour reflecting this settled way of thinking.

These definitions could be summed up by saying:

Attitude is the mental and/or behavioural response you take in any situation.

Generally, most people's attitude consists of habitual or automated responses. Something happens and they respond – automatically, without thinking. This makes sense in some situations. For example, if someone throws a stone at you, you automatically put up your hands to protect your face and eyes. This sort of reflexive response is conditioned into our brains and we have no control over it. It is part of the way our brains are wired – a short circuit that results in a reflex action in times of danger.

Think about what happens if you put your hand on a very hot object such as an oven plate or a boiling kettle. You immediately pull your hand away. You do not say to yourself, 'Gosh this is hot and it will burn my hand, so I'd better pull my hand away.' That thought process would take about five seconds and you would have a badly burnt hand by the time you decided to take action. In contrast, the short circuit in your brain takes half a second to get you to remove your hand and minimise the burning.

It's clear that these reflex responses are extremely useful in

63

times of danger. However, in most other life situations, fast reactions are not useful and may well be very damaging. For instance you are sunbathing near the pool on a warm, sunny day and someone throws a bucket of cold water onto your back. You jump up, see someone holding an empty bucket, and launch a strong verbal attack. If you are really angry you may hit the person. Then sometime later, when you calm down, the person explains that a poisonous spider was on your skin. It could have bitten you. Now, what's your response? Apologies and gratitude, of course.

In most life situations it makes sense to stop and think before acting. As a friend of mine puts it, 'Engage brain before opening mouth.' And once you become aware that, by conscious thinking you can choose your response, then the definition of attitude becomes:

Attitude is the mental and/or behavioural response you choose to take in any situation.

So, by exercising awareness and choice, you can take a large degree of control over how you think and how you behave. Let's put this in simpler language. What shapes your life consists of the circumstances and experiences of your life, how you react to them and how you contribute to them. In my words, the definition could become:

Attitude is an intellectual choice.

I think there are two aspects to attitude:

1. **The amount of control you choose to exercise over your life.**

Some people just drift along and 'go with the flow'. They allow outside circumstances to largely determine their lives. Sometimes this results in a happy life and at other times it does not. In our lives we have the freedom to choose the level of control we wish to exercise over virtually every circumstance we encounter. The degree to which we exercise this choice and control depends on our attitude.

Research shows that people who actively plan their futures lead happier, longer and more meaningful lives than those who do not. We all have this choice. Life planning is an attitude. If *you* do not decide what to do with your life somebody else will.

2. **The way you react to circumstances outside your control and the results of your actions and choices.** As Stephen Covey puts it in *The 7 Habits of Highly Effective People*, 'Between stimulus and response, man has the freedom to choose.' That means the freedom to choose an attitude! It's not what happens to you that counts, it's how you interpret and react to what happens to you that counts. As we are told US football coach Lou Holtz says, 'Life is 10 per cent what happens to me and 90 per cent how I react to it.'

Attitude is a fundamental building block of a happy, meaningful, fulfilled life. The personal challenge is to develop an attitude that will enhance your quality of life, deliver the results (goals, purpose, success) you want, and help you meet your basic human needs that contribute to happiness and fulfilment.

How to Foster an Empowering Attitude

The following is a list of some of the things I have come across that foster an empowering attitude. I'm sure there are many more things you can add. As you read, examine your thinking. Think of examples in your life. Make notes in your Personal Learning Journal. Maybe you need to change some of your attitudes. You will be conscious of any changes you make for a time – until they become second nature and your new way of thinking is automatic. What you are then doing is developing a set of empowering habits (attitudes) that will replace disempowering ones.

Five choices

You always have a choice. Always! This is a fundamental principle of an empowering attitude. There are five **attitude choices** in any situation, especially the situations you do not like. These were covered in Chapter 6, but it's worth repeating them:

1. **Put up with it.** Be critical, full of blame and negative thoughts – but suffer on.

2. **Change the situation** if it's within your power. Do something to improve the situation.

3. **Change your attitude** to the situation. See the positives, the possibilities. Look for a more creative way to be involved.

4. **Get out**! Move onto something else.

5. **Plan** strategically.

Beliefs

Our belief system is the way we see our world and ourselves. If your brain were a computer, then your belief system would be the operating system or software.

Beliefs are mostly a form of attitude. Indeed, many of those who write on the subject use the words 'attitude' and 'belief' interchangeably. However I think that attitude includes other aspects of thinking and behaviour that are not beliefs. As Anton Chekhov put it, 'Man is what he believes.' Personally I would say that attitude is the realisation and awareness that our beliefs are a *choice*. We can change our beliefs if we want to – through our attitude.

No two people view reality in quite the same way. Each of us has been conditioned by our experiences, the way we were reared, our education, the results of our actions and the environment we live in. This conditioning gives each of us our own unique 'software programme' – our belief system. Some of our beliefs limit us and others empower us.

Our attitude will determine how we choose to manage our beliefs. Once we identify and understand our beliefs, we can reinforce the empowering ones and replace the limiting ones. This will help us to really boost achieve our goals.

It's not the events of our lives that shape us, but our beliefs as to what these events mean.

(Anthony Robbins, *Awaken the Giant Within*)

If you believe there are opportunities, you are right. If you believe there are no opportunities, you are also right.

(Henry Ford)

Think positively

Our brains do not know how to put things into negative language. In order to know what *not* to think, our brains have to first think it. Try saying to yourself, 'Don't think of a red bus.' What pops into your head? The red bus. When our brains think of something, we naturally focus on it. Because of this we can end up focusing on what we do *not* want. And very often the result will be that we *get* what we do *not* want.

A good example is the golfer who comes to the fifteenth hole where, on previous occasions, he has hit the water. As he lines up for his shot, he wants to avoid the water. So he thinks in the negative, 'I mustn't land in the water.' The brain focuses on the water and the body follows. Where does the ball go? Into the water.

The much better mental habit (attitude) is to focus on what you *want* to happen, not on what you *do not* want to happen. So the golfer would be far more effective if he thought, 'I'm going to hit the fifteenth green.'

Take your negative thoughts and state them in the positive. For example, instead of telling yourself, 'Don't worry', try telling yourself to 'be alert for opportunities'; or ask yourself, 'How can I best prepare for this challenge?'; or 'How would I like to feel?'

Choose your information

'Garbage in, garbage out!' How true. Our brains are more powerful than the most powerful computer ever built and they store a vast amount of information. This information can, and does, affect how we think and behave. Incoming information can be:

- What you read;

- What you watch;

- What you listen to.

Stand back and think about where the information that enters your brain comes from and how much control you exert over these sources. Most people automatically (in other words, without thinking) listen to the news at least once a day – and you may hear the same news on TV and radio as you read in the papers. What's mostly in 'the news'? Usually a constant stream of negativity endorsed and enhanced by negative journalists and presenters, who believe it is their job to keep you up to date with what's happening in the world.

But their version of 'what's happening' is almost entirely negative – war in Iraq, genocide in Rwanda, death on the roads, rapes, child abuse, economic meltdown, job losses, and on and

68

on. That's a heavy dose of negativity to take in every day, especially morning and evening. By the time you get to work or begin the housework, your mind is already switched to negative mode. Think how this may affect you when you have to handle a difficult customer or a naughty child. If you are in a negative state of mind you might insult the customer or slap your child.

The late-night news can send you to bed full of negative thoughts that leave you worried and disturbed. Not the best recipe for happy dreams and a good night's rest. Far better to go for a short walk and read a good book before turning off the light.

And it's not just the *news* on late-night TV that disturbs us. Research has shown that people who watch TV until lights out tend to have less deep sleep than those who engage in a quiet activity. The problem is that TV tends to be full of shouting, choppy images, crying, flashes, explosions, gunplay, superficial sexuality, bad news, problems and adversity.

William Dement, a US sleep researcher, advises people to go to bed an hour earlier each night and turn off the television no later than an hour before that. The result would be less anxiety and increased happiness and health.

Ann Boylan, the life coach who trained me, advises that we listen to the news just once a day, and preferably at one o'clock. The bad news is less likely to affect you when you are busy in the afternoon. You may get a slight 'downer', but you will be well over it by teatime. Ann says, 'The fact is that we take so much in unconsciously which affects us, both negatively and positively. We may not be consciously aware of the influence the news is having on us, on our mood and behaviour. But it is having an effect.'

In any case, what's so special about the news that we *must* watch or listen to it first thing in the morning and late at night? What's the urgency? How many more people will have been murdered or killed on the roads between 9 a.m. and 1 p.m.? What major life-changing events will you miss if you do not watch the nine o'clock news?

I think we have become addicted to the news and want our three doses a day. This is not good for us. There's just too much negativity there. There's little or no 'good news'. So why not try watching the news just once a day for a week? See if it makes a positive difference to your life.

In *The Progress Paradox*, Gregg Easterbrook says that viewing such disquieting material before nodding off prevents the mind from calming fully before sleep and may inspire nightmares. 'Reading is the ideal before-sleep activity,' he adds.

Focus on the best

As Monty Python's famous Brian said, 'Always look on the bright side of life.' What you focus on is what you will see – and also what you will get. This is beautifully illustrated in the story about the traveller who stopped for fuel at a garage between two towns. He asked the garage owner what sort of people lived in the town he was heading for. 'What were they like in the town you've just come from?' asked the garage owner. 'Very unfriendly and rude,' said the traveller. 'Well, you'll find them exactly the same in the next town,' said the garage owner. The traveller drove on for another night of disappointment with the unfriendly, rude people awaiting him.

A little while later another traveller stopped at the garage and asked the garage owner the same question: 'What sort of people live in the next town?' And the garage owner gave the same response: 'What were they like in the town you have just come from?' The traveller replied; 'I found them very helpful and friendly.' 'Well, you'll find them exactly the same in the next town,' said the garage owner. The traveller drove on for another happy night, with all those friendly, helpful people awaiting him. Same towns, same people – just two different attitudes.

I used to have a very unhelpful attitude towards my fellow drivers. When my friend Michael Murphy and I travelled together, I sometimes use to say that the standard of road etiquette was declining and the number of rude and angry drivers on the road was increasing. Michael's response was to say that he meets many courteous drivers in his travels. Who's right? We probably both are. But who is more relaxed in his driving? Mike is!

In fact it does not matter which one of us is factually correct. The way we choose to interpret the situation strongly affects our thinking and behaviour. I changed my attitude and began to see more examples of courteous driving – and I became more relaxed and courteous myself.

It's the same with people. I believe that the vast majority of people are inherently good. It's their behaviour that makes some of them seem 'bad'. But the behaviour is not the person. You will empower both yourself and other people by focusing on what is good about them, while pointing out (when appropriate) the way in which their behaviour might be adversely affecting themselves, you, other people, and/or the situation everyone is in. Separate the behaviour from the person. In Jesus' words, 'Love the sinner. Hate the sin'.

Free yourself from the disease of finding wrong in others. People who take glee in the pain of others will experience plenty of pain themselves. A really positive thinking habit is to find something to appreciate in any negative person or situation and to develop the habit of giving compliments.

Think before responding

'Engage brain before opening mouth', as they say. This is an incredibly empowering habit. Too often people rush in with inappropriate responses that they later regret. I used to be a classic example of a 'yes-man', saying 'yes' to virtually every request made of me by other people. As a result I took on far too much. The result was that my work and health suffered. It has taken effort to develop a new habit that is encapsulated in a sign that sits on my desk. It says, 'Stop before saying "yes" to avoid frustration, underperformance, stress and sickness.'

When you give yourself space to think before responding, you can choose the best response in relation to your goals, values and mission statement. So develop a habit of saying things like:

☞ I'll come back to you on that.

☞ I need to think this over.

☞ Can we come back to that a little later?

☞ Can we put that on hold?

Choose your associates

My friend Michael Murphy always says, 'Avoid negative people like the plague'. He's right – the people you work and socialise with have an influence on your attitude. Choose them carefully. Choose positive people with values you admire and a high degree of integrity. Be absolutely clear on the people with whom you choose to associate – and those with whom you will not associate. As the saying has it, 'Show me your friends and I'll show you yourself'.

Of course, there will always be times when you are inadvertently in company with people who are engaged in negative, destructive conversation. What attitudinal choices can you make? Well, you can participate in the negativity and knocking. Or you can walk away and talk with someone else. Or you can gently steer the conversation towards something more positive. Or you can get people to focus on solutions rather than problems.

But what about your relatives? It's said that you can chose your friends but you cannot choose your relatives. We all have cousins, aunts, uncles and in-laws who go on and on about the lousy weather, the state of the health service, the neighbours, and so on. A litany of negativity. You may find it difficult to walk away from such people – after all, they are your relatives. But you will know what to expect, so get in first and start the conversation on a positive note.

Ask empowering questions

We are always talking to ourselves, usually unconsciously. This 'talking' often takes the form of questions. For example, when you come to a crossroads it is natural to think, 'Which road will I take?' Another example would be when you are offered a plate of different sandwiches. You look at them and eventually select one. During this selection process, you were unconsciously thinking 'Which sandwich will I like best? The egg mayonnaise, the smoked salmon or the salad?' So thinking is really a system of posing ourselves questions: our brains come up with answers to the questions we ask. The question acts like a trigger for the answer. If this is so, then you can ensure you ask questions that give rise to empowering answers. Develop an attitude of choosing questions that will move you towards solutions and desirable outcomes. Stay away from questions that focus on blame and low-value information.

Take a simple example. Say you're not feeling great: nothing life threatening, just a 'down' feeling. Now choose which question to ask to evaluate the situation so you can decide what action to take:

Question: Why am I feeling so bad?

Answer: I'm not sure. I didn't sleep very well. Maybe I'm worried about my new boss. And there's a big bill for repairing the car coming up. It's affecting me. [Your brain

73

responds to the question and finds reasons for not feeling well: it focuses on the problem and makes it worse.]

Decision: I think I should rest a bit.

Action: I'll take a few days off to 'chill out'.

Result: I may chill out, but the original problem that I perceived (my reality) is still there, and possibly worse. I still feel 'down'.

A better dialogue with yourself might be:

Question: What can I do to feel better?

Answer: I could go for a brisk walk. I know I like that. I could read a good book. I could take my wife to dinner and plan our holidays. [Your brain finds appealing solutions.]

Decision: Book a table for a dinner for two.

Action: Take my wife to dinner. Focus on the holidays.

Result: I forget about the original feeling and feel better.

The simple question has a huge influence on our subsequent thinking, decisions, actions and our resultant feelings. The questions we ask ourselves determine our reality and ultimately, the quality of our lives. By choosing the questions we ask ourselves we can direct and focus our brains to find solutions. The brain responds to the question and finds the answers that best fit the question asked.

So if you ask, 'Why am I always late?', your brain will come up with answers such as, 'That's the way I am', or 'The traffic is always bad', or 'It's difficult getting away from the children', and so on. These answers support the question. The brain is very, very powerful in providing answers. But it can only respond to the question you have asked and the way in which you ask it.

From this it is clear that it is important to choose carefully the questions you ask and harness the brain's power to focus on the positive, constructive aspects of any situation rather than the negative, destructive aspects. If you find yourself in a difficult situation or you are facing a problem, ask empowering, problem-solving questions, such as:

- What can I learn from this?

- What is positive about this problem?

- What is not perfect yet in this situation?

- What am I willing to do to make it the way I want it?

- What if I . . ? [This will open up possibilities.]

- What must I do to . . .? [This links what is possible to the action that's needed to make it happen.]

- What do I want?

- What will I do?

Develop the habit of asking questions that address the things that are good in any situation instead of what's wrong. In other words, 'What do I have?', instead of 'What don't I have?' Focus on solutions not problems.

There is no such thing as failure, only results

This is one of the most powerful attitudinal habits, which I learnt when I did a course on Neuro Linguistic Programming (NLP) run by Julie Silfverberg. I'm sure there have been many times in your life when you have said, 'I've failed . . .' Think of a few and write them in your Personal Learning Journal. Now answer this question for each 'failure': 'Did I set out to fail?' I'm sure you have written 'no' for each so-called 'failure'. The truth is that nobody ever sets out to fail at anything. We all set out with the intention to succeed. However, the results of our actions often do not match our expectations. We call this failure. Worse, we personalise it so that it becomes 'I failed', and damages our self-esteem.

Successful people see undesirable results as the consequence of trying new things that did not give them the results they were after. It's a learning experience. They use what they have learnt, take new actions, and produce new results.

The classic example is Edison's series of experiments to invent an electric light bulb. Apparently, it took about 10,000 attempts! Somewhere along the way – after some 9,000 attempts – a journalist enquired if he was discouraged by 'failing' so many times. Edison responded that he had not failed at all. He had just found many ways that did *not* produce an electric bulb and a number of ways to produce other products. Importantly, Edison did not understand the word 'failure'. He got results – not necessarily the ones he wanted, but they were still results.

Try crossing out the word 'failure' and substituting the words 'result', 'outcome' or 'feedback'. After you have done that, try something different, just like Edison did. In life, many people continue to exhibit the same attitudes and behaviours and expect a different result. And always remember the old saying, 'Insanity can be defined as doing the same thing again and again and expecting a different result.'

The Six Characteristics of a Positive Attitude

The following six characteristics are based on US research carried out using athletes who had made spectacular recoveries from injury – athletes who not only recovered fully, but also moved on to even greater athletic achievement. The research found that these six elements create an unconscious and compelling mental image for success and an assured positive mental attitude.

Characteristic One: Inner motivation
This is to do with moving *towards* a very specific goal and *away from* certain unpleasant consequences. The athletes developed personal, specific and compelling visions of desirable goals or unpleasant consequences. The best athletes used both 'away from' and 'towards' motivation.

Characteristic Two: High standards
The athletes were dedicated to regaining full strength and health. This became their guiding goal, their first and final standard. In addition they had a high inner standard – to be in even better shape than they had been before their injuries.

Characteristic Three: Taking small steps towards a goal
Focusing continuously on the big overall goal can be overwhelming and lead to little progress. The athletes broke the big goal down into very small steps. One athlete had to survive before he could stand, stand before he could walk, and walk again before he could run. Breaking down big goals into more manageable pieces enabled the athletes to focus on small tasks that they could actually do now. They got great satisfaction from completing each small step. Success breeds success.

Characteristic Four: Focusing on the present, with an eye to the future
When concentrating on small tasks and daily tasks, successful athletes (and all people) are focusing on the present moment. Their minds are firmly on what they are doing now. They could be distracted by thinking too far into the future, especially if this raised doubts about recovery.

However, the athletes were also able to think vividly and

fully about a positive future. The attractive, long-term goal pulled them forward, while they solidly maintained their motivation in the present. If we use this tactic, we find that it becomes easier to accept the short-term pains and setbacks. At the same moment that you are concentrating on achieving the small task at hand, you can still see the big, bright picture of your future accomplishment drawing you forward.

Characteristic Five: Personal involvement

The more that the athletes actively participated in their own rehabilitation plans, the more they helped themselves – and this, in turn, greatly improved their chances of full recovery. It would have been easier for the athletes to place themselves passively in the hands of experts. But the research indicates that this approach would have been a mistake. Athletes, and the rest of us, need to work actively with our highly trained experts to produce the results we want.

Taking action in our own life – however small that action – is important. Taking action ensures that we are *part* of the process and, when we participate, we influence what is occurring. Involvement increases our personal commitment and focuses our intensity.

Characteristic Six: Self-to-self comparisons

The really successful athletes looked solely at their own progress. They did not compare themselves to other athletes or to other people's expectations. They made 'self-to-self' comparisons. This means that they compared the place they had started from with the place where they currently found themselves. They asked continually, 'How far have I come since yesterday, last week, last month?'

The opposite is usually the case in our society. Our culture endorses comparison with the performance of others – 'self-to-others' comparisons. This happens in school, work and play. It happens in education, sport and the workplace. While there is merit in using successful people as models, it can be very counterproductive to continually compare your own progress and performance to that of others.

The reality may be that 'so-and-so' is inherently a faster runner, or a faster thinker than you are, and so you will find it impossible to match his or her performance. At this point you might conclude that you are not good enough and are unlikely to achieve your goal. The opposite might also be true – you may be an inherently better runner and a faster thinker than 'so-and-so'. If you aspire to his or her level of achievement you may fail to reach any higher, and this can extinguish the creative joy of accomplishment that encouraged a very young Picasso, the slow maths student Albert Einstein, and the basketball superstar Michael Jordan to exceed themselves again and again.

The Glass is Always Half-full

There is an interesting half-full/ half-empty story that concerns two shoe salesmen who, over forty years ago, went by boat to Nigeria to assess the market there. Both disembarked at Lagos and spent some time on their market research. One clear fact emerged. Nobody wore shoes in Nigeria.

In the days before mobile phones and the Internet, the first salesman sent back a telegram to his company: 'Nobody wears shoes [stop] No market [stop] Arrive back next ship [stop].'

The second salesman also sent a telegram to his company: 'Nobody wears shoes [stop] Major market opportunity [stop] Send out shipload of shoes immediately [stop]'

Within a short time the second salesman had developed the Nigerian market and his company, Bata, had gained almost 100 per cent control of the young market that continued to grow and grow. Eventually the name 'Bata' became synonymous with shoes in Nigeria in the same way that 'Hoover' has become synonymous with vacuum cleaners.

What happened? Two experienced salesmen arrived in the same place and observed the same set of circumstances. Yet the two came to totally different conclusions. One saw opportunity, the other saw none. One saw a half-empty glass; the other a half-full glass. They had different attitudes and their attitudes had a major influence on subsequent events.

PART THREE:

THE LIFE PLANNING TOOLKIT

CHAPTER 9: THE STRATEGIC LIFE PLANNING PROCESS

The Reactive or Proactive Life

What Are the Three Ws?
(PLJ Exercise Self-assessment Process 6: Consistent goal achievement)

Using the Three Ws to Plan Your Life
W1: Where do I want to be?; W2: Where am I now?;
W3: What will I do when I get where I want to be?;
The nature of change; Using the Three W Process to
manage change.

CHAPTER 10: SYSTEMATIC AND CREATIVE GOAL ACHIEVEMENT

Systematic Planning
Systematic fixed planning; Systematic responsive
planning; Systematic flexible planning.

Creative Planning
The 'unexpected' in your life (PLJ Exercise Self-assessment Process 7: What role have planning and the 'unexpected' played in my life?); The 'unconscious' in your life; Harnessing the 'unconscious' and the 'unexpected'.

Applying the Three Ws Process to Creative Goal Achievement

CHAPTER 11: THE GOAL-SETTING PROCESS

Describing a Vivid and Specific Goal
(PLJ Exercise: Goal-setting Process 1: Check your goal for purpose); Check for alternative goals; W1: How to write your goal using the SMART process (PLJ Exercise Goal-setting Process 2: My likes and dislikes); W2: Describing where you are now (PLJ Exercise Goal-setting Process 3: Where do I want to be and where am I now?); W3: What am I going to do to get where I want to be? (PLJ Exercise Goal-setting Process 4: What kind of goal am I setting?).

What Else Can I Do to Maximise the Probability of Achieving My Goals?
Tackle positive and negative beliefs about your goal; The path to your goal.

CHAPTER 12: FINDING YOUR GOALS

Measuring Your Overall Happiness
    (PLJ Exercise Self-assessment Process 8: Life satisfaction ratings chart)

The Balanced Goal-setting Process
    (PLJ Exercise Goal-setting Process 5: Choosing your goals); Decide on the most important areas of your life (AoLs); Prioritise these areas; Score your current level of satisfaction in each area (PLJ Exercise Self-assessment Process 9: AoL satisfaction ratings); How balanced is your life? (PLJ Exercise Self-assessment Process 10: The Wheel of Life); Select three areas of life in which to set goals; Use the Three W Process to set goals ((PLJ Exercise: Goal-setting Process 6: Setting goals); Schedule the actions to achieve the goals; 'Walk the talk'; Measure progress regularly; Continue to set goals that lift satisfaction scores (PLJ Exercise Self-assessment Process 11: Monitoring progress).

Areas of Life: a More Detailed Approach
    Relationships; Career.

Maintaining Balance

CHAPTER 13: LIVE LONGER, LIVE HEALTHIER

Calendar Age, Physical Age and Psychological Age
    What is your physical age? What is your psychological age? Conclusion.

CHAPTER 14: LIFETIME MANAGEMENT

Basic Principles

LifeTime Management in Practice
  The 'big picture'; Detailed time organisation.

CHAPTER 15: THE INNER YOU

What are My Values?
  (PLJ Exercise Self-assessment Process 12: Areas of Life)

Fundamental Human Needs
  Understanding human needs: Maslow's hierarchy of human needs; William Glasser; Griffin and Tyrell.

Your Path to Self-Actualisation

CHAPTER 16: QUESTIONS ARE THE ANSWER
(PLJ Exercise Personal Mission Statement 1)

CHAPTER 17: PUTTING IT ALL TOGETHER
(PLJ Exercise: Personal Mission Statement 2)

EPILOGUE: WHERE NEXT?

CHAPTER 9

THE STRATEGIC LIFE PLANNING PROCESS

'WOULD YOU TELL ME, PLEASE, WHICH WAY I OUGHT TO WALK
FROM HERE?' ASKED ALICE.
'THAT DEPENDS A GOOD DEAL ON WHERE YOU WANT TO GET
TO,' SAID THE CAT.
'I DON'T MUCH CARE WHERE,' SAID ALICE.
'THEN IT DOESN'T MATTER WHICH WAY YOU WALK,' SAID THE
CAT.

(LEWIS CARROLL, *ALICE'S ADVENTURES IN WONDERLAND*)

The Reactive or Proactive Life

Many, if not most, people live in an unplanned, reactive way.
Reactive people usually only make decisions when something
happens to them: they react to present circumstances rather
than planning ahead and setting goals. Sometimes their reactive
decisions have positive results and sometimes they have negative
results. Reactive people tend to focus on problems, not
solutions. For them, life is a bit of a lottery.

The most reactive type of person might say, 'Life's a bitch.
I don't like where I am and I haven't a clue where I want to go!

I seem to have problems most of the time.' People who think like this live from crisis to crisis: the crisis may be big or small, but it is always crisis that prompts decisions. Their decisions are 'away-from' decisions: based on the desire to escape unfavourable circumstances. This type of decision-making is without direction (goals) and so the results swing wildly from beneficial to very damaging. Reactive, 'away-from' decisions are often based on negative emotions like fear and anxiety, and often enough the reactive person will jump 'out of the frying pan, into the fire'.

There is another sort of reactive person who has a few, vague goals, and may say of his or her life, 'I know I want to be happy and sometimes I am. But life can be difficult and I get by, somehow.' Such a person has a 'go-with-the-flow' or a 'happy-go-lucky' sort of life that just 'happens'. Sometimes it happens to be good and sometimes it is difficult, but life is always living the person: the person is not living the life.

Proactive people, on the other hand, believe in planning. They do not wait for something to happen to them before making decisions. Instead they think about the future and make plans for moving towards the future they desire. When negative things happen, they focus on solutions not the problem. 'Towards' motivation is based on positive emotions like desire, happiness and love.

Proactivity is the essence of strategic planning. Strategic means that you establish a desired goal or outcome and then work towards that outcome. Strategic planning is using careful planning to work out how to get to that goal or outcome.

What are the Three Ws?

Successful people in all areas of life are proactive. They proactively make decisions and take actions to achieve goals that result in positive changes in their own lives, whether in relationships, career or finances. I am assuming that you choose to be a proactive player in your own life, and so the remainder of this chapter explores the theory and practice of consistent goal achievement.

SELF-ASSESSMENT PROCESS 6:
CONSISTENT GOAL ACHIEVEMENT

Think about how consistent goal achievement might apply in your own life and write these two questions in your Personal Learning Journal:

1. Have you ever set a goal and achieved it?

2. Have you ever set a goal and failed to achieve it?

I expect that, like most people, you answered 'yes' to both questions. Write that down and think about it – the issue is not 'Can I achieve a goal?' You have already shown that you can. The issue is how to go about achieving goals *consistently*, so that when you set a goal you have a 90 per cent or more chance of achieving it.

I believe that the goal-achieving process I now describe will enable you to consistently achieve your goals. I'm going to cover it in the following steps:

- A brief description of the empowering Three Ws Process.

- A discussion of the nature of change.

- How you can use the three Ws to manage change in your own life.

- How you can harness the power of your conscious and unconscious mind.

Using the Three Ws Process to Plan your Life

The objective of strategic life planning is to get what you want out of life in every area. The Three Ws Process is a self-questioning process you can use to construct a realistic life plan. Ask yourself the crucial Three W questions for life planning, noticing the ways in which each question can enable you.

W^1 Where do I want to be?	Future Vision Provides direction Establishes long-term goals
W^2 Where am I now?	Current reality Realistic self-assessment
W^3 What will I do to get where I want to be?	Short-term goals Decisions Actions

Table 2

W^1: Where do I want to be?

Stephen Covey puts it very well when he describes the second habit in *The 7 Habits of Highly Effective People*: 'Begin with the end in mind.' Imagine you are getting into a taxi – what is the first question the driver will ask you? 'Where do you want to go?' Imagine just saying, 'I don't know – let's just go!' Look back to Lewis Carroll's delightful nonsense exchange between the cat and Alice, which introduced this chapter. I think you will see that the driver will probably react like the cat when approached by Alice at the crossroads.

The question 'Where do you want to go?' (or 'to be', 'to have' or 'to do') is posed to you every moment of your life. And

'What do I want?' is probably the most powerful question that you should ask yourself whenever you are making decisions in a planned way. This is what **W¹** is all about:

- envisioning the life you want to create;

- giving direction to your life;

- setting clear goals;

- finding answers and solutions.

W²: Where am I now?

This is fairly obvious: you must know where you are starting. Imagine ringing a taxi firm and saying, 'I need a taxi to take me to the airport.' When the taxi driver enquires where you are, you reply, 'Uh, uh . . . I don't know!' Will the taxi arrive? No way.

W² describes where you are now in relation to what you want of the future. This is the starting point at which you make the decisions and take the actions that move you towards your goal.

W³: 'What will I do to get where I want to be?'

This is where the action begins. This is the 'taxi' – the vehicle that gets you from where you are now to where you want to be: from A to B, from **W²** to **W¹**.

W³ is the step in the process that enables you to achieve the goals you set and to create a life you enjoy living. It involves examining options, making decisions (choosing what you think are the best options), and being very aware of the consequences of your actions. At first glance, **W³** appears fairly straightforward: you know where you want to go and you also know where you are now. So just plan the route, set off in the right direction, and you will get there. Right? Perhaps, but, as we all know, life is rarely simple. How can using the Three Ws to actively set life goals help you negotiate the twists and turns on the road?

The nature of change

The world and your environment are always changing. We also change, whether we like it or not: we get older, form new relationships, form new beliefs, change career, get sick, get well, and so on. Everything is changing, growing, declining, stagnating, and dying. Change is a constant. Moreover, change creates more change. In all situations, when you do something (initiate change), this precipitates further changes. The life planning landscape is not stable – rather, it is like a trampoline. When you move, the trampoline surface and everything on it moves too. It is like when you drop a stone into a pond: the surface of the water ripples and everything floating on it begins to bob up and down. The changes we make through our decisions and actions always have consequences. Your objective is to bring about change that helps you achieve your life goals.

Using the Three Ws Process to manage change

Life planning using the Three Ws is all about deciding on the kind of life you want to live and managing change so as to create that life. You take an active part in your future: you make it happen. The alternative is to leave everything to chance and to 'go with the flow'. You may end up rich, poor, healthy, unhealthy, happy or miserable. It will be your choice. If you do choose to 'go with the flow', I wish you the best of luck – but always remember that it is you who have given over control of your life to pressures outside yourself and unforeseen events.

However, you still have – and will never lose – the opportunity to take control of your life and to choose active involvement in creating the life you want. One of my own life goals is to encourage others down this path, using the Three W Process to carve out their own futures.

As you read on, assume that you have already envisioned a

clear, well-described goal for the future. The logical process for setting yourself goals will be covered in Chapter 12, but for now I would like you to develop an understanding of what can happen when you set up such a clear goal: this understanding of the powerful changes that clear goals bring about in your life is a wonderful motivator in itself.

CHAPTER 10

SYSTEMATIC AND CREATIVE
GOAL ACHIEVEMENT

GOALS ARE THE FUEL THAT POWER SUCCESS IN LIFE.

(CON HURLEY)

Systematic Planning

Imagine that, after much thinking and writing, you are now clear on what your goal is (W^1) and where you are now in relation to that goal (W^2). At this stage you must begin to do something: make a decision, choose an option, and take the actions that will move you towards achieving your goal. How do you do that? Remember that a goal without action is just a dream, no matter how clearly you describe it. Action is always needed. How will you know which actions to take?

First, look again at the description of your goal. Imagine that you have achieved the goal and that you can express it in the present tense, then ask this question: 'What steps have led me to the achievement of this goal?' Think back over the time it took to achieve the goal and all the actions and steps that ensured that the goal was achieved. You will usually find yourself in one of three situations. You will have:

1. total clarity about the steps you took to achieve the goal;

2. clarity on one or two steps, but you may be unsure of what happened next; or you may have

3. no idea of how the goal was achieved!

Systematic Fixed Planning

Imagine that your goal is to build the house of your dreams. You start by getting an architect to design your dream home. This is W^1: drawings, plans and diagrams that clearly and precisely show the goal – the house – in total clarity. You are also absolutely clear on where you are now (W^2): you have a site with planning permission, a set of plans and a builder.

So you look at the plans of your finished home and ask the question, 'What has to happen to achieve this goal – to get my house built?' The answers jump out: foundations are laid; walls are built; the roof goes on; windows go in; walls are plastered; services are installed – water, electricity, phone, and so on; floors are laid; the house is decorated; a kitchen is installed; furniture is delivered; the entrance and garden are completed; and finally you move in!

This is a straightforward, step-by-step process, one step leading naturally to the next. You know with certainty that when the walls are built, the roof goes on next, and so on. This goal-achieving process is easy to predict and I call it **Systematic Fixed Planning**. You set up a system, follow the steps, take the pre-planned actions and your house is built – your goal is achieved. Little or nothing changes to modify the actions needed to complete the project: even if there is a problem with the arrival of materials so that the process is delayed, the steps remain the same.

Systematic fixed planning works extremely well when all

the steps to reach the goal are known in advance. It works well when working with anything to do with widgets – inanimate objects not subject to human emotions and events outside your control. The assembly line is the classic example of systematic fixed planning. That was the means by which Henry Ford revolutionised car manufacturing, so that today cars, computers, washing machines are all manufactured by a process that utilises this planning method.

This is also what young Jack is doing when he builds a model airplane, car or train engine: he starts with the picture on the box (W^1); next he gets out all the components, glue and tubes of paints (W^2); then he follows the diagrams and instructions and takes the steps to build the model (W^3). The finished Spitfire on a shelf in Jack's bedroom is a perfect example of a simple and effective planning process that can be repeated time after time.

However this kind of planning and management only works where there are few, if any, outside influences on the creative process. Under these circumstances, you are almost 100 per cent certain that step 1 leads to step 2, and so on, until you inevitably reach your goal.

Systematic Responsive Planning

Most life planning situations are not simple – just as you take a step towards your goal, other factors may change, in the same way as there are physical changes on the surface of the trampoline when your body moves. The changes that occur may be owing to:

- your own action;

- a change in events outside your control; or

- new information that changes your goal.

For example, take Michael, who plans to sail his yacht from

Cork in Ireland to Santander in northern Spain. He has taken a navigation course, so he knows his stuff. He gets out the charts and uses a compass to set his direction at 180° due south. He takes account of the tides, wind direction and speed and ends up with a line on the map and the compass direction to follow, then he sets off. Does Michael arrive in Santander eighteen hours later, saying '*buenos días*' to the harbour master?

Well, yes, he does – if everything remains the same. But winds have an annoying habit of changing, especially in that unpredictable piece of the Atlantic where the Celtic Sea merges into the Bay of Biscay. For example, look at what would happen if the winds went from north to west after six hours at sea. Instead of '*buenos días*' in Santander, Michael would be greeted with a '*bonjour*' in Brest, France. And, even worse, if the winds swung east, after eighteen hours Michael would find himself out in the Atlantic heading for the icebergs off Newfoundland. Instead of responding with a '*buenos días*' or '*bonjour*', Michael is likely to find himself saying, 'oh sh . . .!'

In practice, of course, this does not often happen, because the experienced sailor is continuously monitoring his position and changing direction as needed. So, if he finds he is heading towards France or Canada, he alters course to bring him back on line for his goal, in this case Santander. In other words, W^2 is constantly changing, so he must keep a constant eye on his actual position as well as his destination (W^1), adjusting direction in the face of the changes around him.

This goal-achieving process is less easy to predict and I call it **Systematic Responsive Planning**. Initially, you are as clear as possible about W^1 and W^2. You take actions (W^3) that will move you towards your goal, monitor what happens, get new information and then take new steps to move towards your original goal. The steps can be summed up as follows:

1. Set the goal;

2. determine where you are;

3. take planned action – only one step;

4. monitor results of action – feedback;

5. plan and take new action.

Systematic Flexible Planning

Another variation of systematic planning works well when you are unable to deduce some or all of the steps needed to achieve your goal. Many people dislike this. They want certainty and like to know in advance all the things they need to do to achieve a goal. This is not always possible and it can be very frustrating and unproductive to imagine every step towards a desired goal before one begins to take action. In fact, many people never start the goal-achieving process because of this uncertainty. They are afraid to take one step because they do not know what to do after that. They remain frozen like a rabbit in the headlights.

This is where **Systematic Flexible Planning** comes in. Again, clarity on W^1 and W^2 is needed. Next you take a small step in the direction of your goal. Then pause, monitor feedback and select the next step. You cannot see all the steps and actions you need to take, but you know you are going in the right direction. One step builds on the next and you eventually achieve your goal.

It's a bit like Pedro, driving from Cork to Dublin in the dark with no map (plan), very little knowledge of Ireland, and no signposts for Dublin (we ensured they were all removed for this illustration). He knows W^1 and W^2, but W^3 is largely a mystery. He also knows that Dublin is in a general northeast direction, so he buys a compass and heads that way. On the road, Pedro stops at a garage (which does not sell maps!) and asks for directions. A Polish attendant points and Pedro motors on only to find the road blocked after 40 miles. He has now learnt that it helps to take advice from local people who know the roads, so he turns back and stops at a pub. The barman gives him directions across country roads to reach the main Cork–Dublin road. After a series of similar adventures and learning experiences, Pedro arrives in Dublin – his goal, W^1.

Looking back on the journey he knows that it was impossible to predict his route. But he achieved his goal by:

- taking some action towards his goal;

- getting new information by asking directions;

- acting on this information;

- learning from the results and experiences; and

- repeating the process until he reached his destination.

Creative Planning

All three variations on the systematic planning process that we have just looked at work at the conscious, logical level of your mind and are widely used by business managers. They also work well for many individual goals. However, the individual has two additional, very powerful, tools that businesses rarely have:

- the power of the unconscious; and

- the ability to recognise serendipity in life – those mysteries that we will call 'external, unexplained and unexpected help'.

By tapping into these hidden assets, the individual can hugely increase his or her chances of successful goal achievement. This is another variation on the kind of 'towards' motivation and goal-setting that we encountered earlier, favoured by proactive people. Although highly unpredictable, it is also very creative and flexible – and, amazingly, highly successful. Let's call it **Creative Goal Achievement**. The key factors are:

- a seriously specific description of the goal – verbal, written and visualised;

- a strong belief and expectation that the goal will come to fruition;

- a strong belief and expectation that opportunities will arise;

- heightened awareness to identify these opportunities;

- the ability to trust in intuition while making decisions.

In the three systematic approaches, everything is done consciously and logically. In creative goal achievement the unconscious is also brought into action. This is why awareness is so important. Your unconscious will identify opportunities by bringing them to your conscious attention, and you must use your awareness to see that they are what you need to move towards your goal.

The 'unexpected' in your life

SELF-ASSESSMENT PROCESS 7:

WHAT ROLE HAVE PLANNING AND THE 'UNEXPECTED' PLAYED IN MY LIFE?

Consider first the way in which all the various aspects of your life have evolved. The most important areas of your life are likely to be:

- relationships;

- health;

living environment;

friends;

career;

money.

Look at this list and, for each area, consider:

1. Where are you now?

2. When you look back how much systematic planning do you see?

3. What other factors influenced where you are now?

> Note the answers to these questions in your Personal Learning Journal and write down some specific examples as well.

> I strongly suspect that you will find that there are a huge number of 'unplanned' factors that have influenced where you are now. You might characterise these as: chance; luck, good or bad; being in the right (or wrong) place at the time; coincidence; fate; chance; and intuition. Now make sure that you have included examples of these 'chance' events while you are recording what has brought you to this stage in your life.

After you have completed this exercise, the chances are you will be feeling that your life is very unpredictable and curiously influenced by things that you cannot explain or plan for – but that nevertheless have played a huge part in bringing you to your current experience of living. Whatever you want to call these chance events, I would like to pose these questions:

1. Are these events random and totally outside your control? If so, do you just plan as best you can and ride your luck through life, taking advantage of the 'good luck' events and coping as best you can with the 'bad luck' events?

2. Or should you try to have at least some kind of plan – is there a way in which you can influence these chance events in order to maximise the amount of good luck and opportunity that comes into your life?

3. Could you go even further and actually *create* your own luck – actually *bring* luck into your life?

To answer these questions I want to examine the role that our minds play in goal-setting. We have already seen that we use our minds in systematic planning – but in fact we are only using that part of the mind that we are aware of, our *conscious* mind. We use analysis, planning and logic to make plans, then we take the necessary steps and monitor results to achieve our goals. However there is another part of our minds that can turbocharge the goal-achievement process – the *unconscious* mind. Let's see how this works.

The 'unconscious' in your life

Information from your living environment comes into your mind primarily through your five senses – sight, sound, touch, smell and taste. It is estimated that some two million pieces of information come into your mind every second. Two million! You would be mentally overwhelmed if all the information coming into your mind through your five senses was in your conscious thoughts – so much that you might shut down with information overload. If you stop for a second and examine your environment, you will probably notice things that were not registering until now – the sound of the radio, the smell of paint, the touch of your thighs on the chair, the colour of the curtains and the saliva in your mouth. You may even salivate as you begin to 'pay attention'.

Suddenly you are aware of factors of which you were previously *unconscious*. What has happened is that while you were reading your unconscious mind only brought to your awareness those things on which you *consciously* decided to focus. At the moment, I am aware of what I am writing, the keypad and the computer screen. Everything else is filtered out by my unconscious mind. But if I stop for a moment, I notice I'm wearing a green cardigan, there's a glass of water on my desk – and probably many other factors that I do not need to focus on for the important job I have in hand. Try it – and be aware that:

- your **unconscious mind** screens out what you do not need to be aware of; and

- your **unconscious mind** lets through information that you need to be aware of.

Your unconscious mind is, in effect, acting as if it were the tuner or band selector on a radio. There are millions of radio waves coming into your radio through the aerial. If they all came through the speaker you would hear an unintelligible babble. But you use the tuner to focus on Lyric FM and the tuner allows the signals for Lyric in and screens out all the other signals coming into the radio. Your unconscious mind is like that tuner on the radio, selecting what is appropriate in your current situation and screening out everything else.

When you set a clear goal it's as if you are adjusting the 'tuner' in your unconscious. Shortly, I will describe a process that allows your conscious mind to prepare a set of clear instructions for your unconscious. These instructions tell your unconscious to be alert for any information that is relevant to your goal. So, when your unconscious is monitoring all the information coming in through your five senses, it will bring to your awareness information that will help you achieve your goal. In effect, your conscious mind is the goal-setter and your unconscious mind is the goal-getter. Here are some examples of how the unconscious mind works as a goal-getter.

Most of us have experienced deciding to buy a specific product and then 'suddenly' seeing unusually high numbers of these products every day. For example when you decide to buy a new car you will probably choose a make, model and colour – perhaps a red Toyota Corolla. Immediately you may find that you began to notice more and more of this make, model and colour on the road. Did Toyota suddenly make more red Corollas and improve their sales in your area? No, they were always there, but your unconscious brought them to your attention because you had consciously decided this was the type of car you wanted. Before you set that goal, your unconscious screened out all the red Corollas.

When I was deciding on a new career some years ago, I could not describe it precisely. I was clear that it should involve helping people to successfully plan their lives. Then one day I was rapidly turning the last pages in the *Irish Examiner* and something caught my eye in the small ads, although I do not normally read them. It was an ad for a Diploma Course in Life and Business Coaching. I rang the number, met Ann Boylan (the course presenter), signed on for the course and became a life coach. It fitted exactly the description of the new career I wanted – helping people to successfully plan their lives.

This was my unconscious mind at work, although I did not realise it at the time: I had consciously considered my goal and my unconscious selected the piece of information that helped me achieve it. Without my conscious clarity of goal I doubt very much that I would have spotted the ad, since my unconscious would have screened it out with the hundreds of other ads on that page.

Harnessing the 'unconscious' and the 'unexpected'

When your unconscious receives clear instructions in the form of a clear, written goal, it acts like a radio receiver and tunes into all the information that is relevant to your goal. You are more focused on what you want. This allows you to spot opportunities and ways that will help you achieve your goal. We know that all the radio waves come from radio transmitters and satellites. There is no mystery there, just as there is no mystery to the red Toyota Corollas or the ad for the Life Coaching Course. They were always there, but you and I were not aware of them until we had set specific goals and our heightened unconscious picked up the signals relevant to these goals.

But what about the unexplained, unexpected happenings that come along just when you need them – the serendipities that life supplies? They are often referred to as luck, coincidences, or miracles. There are legions of 'good luck' and 'amazing coincidence' stories that cannot be rationally explained. An interview with Warren Buffett in *Fortune* magazine told of the important role luck had played in his early career. When he was twenty he was rejected by Harvard Business School. He went to the library to check out other business schools and his attention was caught by the names of two Columbia business professors that he admired. Buffett applied to Columbia at the last minute and was accepted. One of the professors later became Buffett's mentor and helped initiate his highly successful career in business. As Buffett later remarked, 'Probably the luckiest thing that ever happened to me was getting rejected from Harvard'.

So, what's going on here? I'm not sure, except to say that there is a growing body of thought and evidence to suggest that there is 'something else out there' that works with us to achieve our goals. The quote from W. H. Murray that introduces chapter 3 clearly describes this phenomenon: the occasion when one firmly commits and 'Providence moves too', resulting in 'unforeseen incidents and meetings and material assistance . . .' That 'something else out there' has been given various other names:

Universal Unconscious	Super-conscious
Higher Self	The Secret
SynchroDestiny	The Power of Intention
The Law of Attraction	The Holographic Universe
Creative Tension	God

Table 3

This is not the place to discuss what the 'something else out there' might be. What is vitally important and relevant is that, as Murray puts it, 'The moment one definitely commits oneself, then Providence moves too'. In other words, unexplained, external factors can help you achieve your goals. At this stage, I'm not too concerned as to why, or even how, this happens. I am more interested in whether or not each one of us can learn to use these unexplained factors to achieve goals. The answer, I believe, is yes. You do not need to believe in miracles, the universal unconscious or God to do this. The only thing you need to know is that it works and then begin to ask, 'How can I make it work for me?'

Applying the Three Ws Process to Creative Goal Achievement

We have seen that your conscious mind is really only the tip of

104

the iceberg that is your thinking mind. You can tap into the incredible power of your unconscious mind and 'whatever else is out there' every time you:

- clearly describe your goal (W^1) in a way that communicates your wants to your goal-getter – the unconscious;

- support your goal through your current feelings and beliefs (W^2);

- seize the opportunities that present themselves to you – take action (W^3);

- increase your awareness of the unexpected when it occurs. This should be your prompt to say, 'That's interesting, how can I use this to help me achieve my goal?'; and

- begin to trust your intuition or 'gut feelings' when making decisions.

As well as providing a clear structure for systematic planning, the Three Ws Process can also be used to harness the power of your unconscious and 'the external, unexplained, unexpected help' that is available to aid you in achieving your goals. We can use W^1 and W^2 to describe goals in ways that open up all avenues of help – W^3 will incorporate awareness and intuition to pick up what is coming from your unconscious and 'elsewhere'.

In contrast to the systematic planner, the creative planner initially focuses more on W^1, or on describing where they want to be. He or she puts a huge emphasis on describing the goal and giving it attention – writing it, visualising it, talking about it. The description of W^2 is fairly straightforward. W^3 – the answers to 'What am I going to do to get there?' – are a combination of systematic and unexpected decisions and actions. In addition, creative goal achievement places emphasis on emotions (feelings) and beliefs and these are spread throughout the Three Ws.

To sum up, the creative goal achiever has:

1. a seriously specific description of the goal. This description can be written, painted or sketched, and even portrayed by a collage technique (perhaps assembling an assort-ment of images from magazines and news-papers that express your goal in visual terms);

2. a strong belief and expectation that the goal will come to fruition;

3. a strong belief and expectation that opportunities will arise;

4. heightened awareness to identify these opportunities; and

5. trust in his or her intuition to make the right decisions and choose the right opportunities.

CHAPTER 11:

THE GOAL-SETTING PROCESS

YOUR CONSCIOUS MIND IS THE GOAL-SETTER; YOUR
UNCONSCIOUS MIND IS THE GOAL-GETTER.

(ANON)

Describing a Vivid and Specific Goal

This is the first and most crucial part of all forms of goal achievement. The objective is to make the goal vivid and real to: 1) your conscious; 2) your unconscious; and 3) 'whatever else' is 'out there' to help you. I am going to describe how to express your goal in words and pictures that will harness help from all three sources. But why is writing a goal so important? This is clearly illustrated in a study carried out on 1970 business studies graduates of Yale University. Each graduate was asked about their level of goal commitment (see the table below). Then twenty years later the graduates were interviewed about their progress in life. The results were clear:

Level of Goal	% of class	Financial State in 1990
Specific written goals	3 %	Very wealthy
Specific unwritten goals	10 %	Well off
Vague goals	60 %	Getting by
No goals	27 %	Needing financial help

Table 4: Results of a Study of the Yale University Business Class of 1970

Some of the main conclusions of the study were as follows:

🖙 In terms of money (wealth), the 13 per cent of people who set specific goals were far better off than people who had vague or no goals.

🖙 In terms of quality of life, people who set specific goals had happier marriages, fewer divorces and a generally better quality of life than those who did not set goals. It is worth noting that 80 per cent of divorces are attributed to financial problems.

🖙 It is important to draw attention to the distinction between written and unwritten goals. People who had specific written goals were the better off in all measures of wealth and quality of life. In fact, the total wealth of the 3 per cent who had specific, written goals was more than the combined wealth of the other 97 per cent! So, having **specific** goals is important and having **specific, written** goals is more important still.

The reason why written goals are achieved more often than unwritten goals is to do with your unconscious and what we are calling the 'unexpected'. Your unconscious mind seems to rely on clarity and detail. Registering your goals as unwritten thoughts and ideas is good: the thinking process involved will communicate your goals to your unconscious. But when you write (and paint, draw, or collage) something down on paper, you are setting up more than one communication channel between your conscious and your unconscious mind. The act of recording the goals can be seen as a three-step process:

1. When you write, you see your goal on paper so you are **communicating visually** with your unconscious. This visual representation of your goal is enhanced when you draw or paint it.

2. As you write, you feel the pen and the paper. This feeling is **kinaesthetic** communication with your unconscious.

2. As you write, thoughts are going through your head as **internal talk** and ideas – you set up an internal dialogue with yourself.

So writing does a far better job of imprinting your goal in your unconscious than just thinking about it. And the way you write your goal is also important. The language you use to express the goal operates on three levels:

1. It gives an extremely clear, conscious, description of your goal.

2. It communicates your goal to your unconscious in ways that activate your unconscious to spot and bring opportunities to your awareness.

3. It engenders positive feelings about your goal. These feelings and emotions give energy to your goal and this energy attracts unexpected opportunities, luck and coincidences.

Before I describe in more detail *how* to write your goals so that you consistently achieve them, there are two further steps that will help you ensure that you are working on goals that are right for you.

GOAL-SETTING PROCESS 1:
CHECK YOUR GOAL FOR PURPOSE

This should be done early in the goal-setting process and perhaps again when you have set your goal. The objective is to ensure that the goal fits in with your overall identity and purpose in life as described in Chapter 16. Examine your written goal and ask these questions:

- What is the purpose of this goal? ('I want this goal so that . . .')

- What is my intention with this goal?

- What will this goal do for me?

- What will this goal give me?

- Write down the answers to each of these questions in your Personal Learning Journal. You can refer to the answers as you go back and check your goal.

- When you feel your answers are comprehensive, ask yourself, 'Am I happy with the ultimate purpose of this goal?' If your answer is 'yes' then this is a real goal for you, a goal that will move you towards what you ultimately want in life.

Check for alternative goals

You have checked your goal for purpose and you are that happy it fits in with your overall life purpose. Well done – but are there other goals that would achieve the same purpose? Other goals that would be easier, suit you better, or have better consequences? Here are four ways to look for alternative goals.

- Ask yourself, 'What other goals would achieve this purpose?'

- Brainstorm with others.

- Get help from a group – friends, discussion group, relations.

- Talk to a coach or mentor for advice.

For example, imagine that your first goal is to get to Dublin, with the ultimate goal of seeing a big match. Before you examine ways of getting to Dublin (by car, train, air) ask yourself if there are there any other ways to achieve your ultimate goal, which is to see the big match. An obvious alternative would be to watch it on TV at home, in a club or pub.

W^1: How to write your goal using the SMART process

When you begin to write your goal, you should remember that it is important to:

- give a clear, easily understood description of your goal;

- make your goal real to your unconscious mind;

- make the goal believable; and

- engender positive, exciting feelings about your goal.

A commonly used structure for writing goals is based on the **SMART** process, which I have altered slightly to stand for:

Specific;

Measurable;

'As of now' (the goal is expressed in the present tense);

Responsible;

Towards what I want (the goal is expressed positively).

SPECIFIC

Vagueness gives uncertain and unsatisfactory results. You need to state your goal as specifically as possible. Specificity is essential for both systematic and creative goal achievement. You have to clearly instruct your *unconscious* mind in the outcome that you *consciously* want. The more precise this instruction is, the better the chance of achieving the goal. So state exactly what you want. Look at what you write and ask yourself, 'If what I have written was in front of me right now, would I recognise it as what I want?'

For example, say you write as your goal: 'I want more money.' You win €100 on the lottery. That fits your goal of wanting more money. But is that what you really wanted? So state your true goal clearly and precisely, for instance, 'I want to have €30,000 to invest in 2010.' I know a woman who actually set that goal in January and had achieved it by March.

MEASURABLE

How will you know if you are moving towards your goal? How will you know that you have achieved your goal? What must you see, feel or hear to know you have achieved your goal? How will you measure success? This is tied in with how specific you have been in describing your goal. The more specific your goal, the more measurable progress and successful achievement will be.

'As of Now'

Goals expressed in the future have lower chances of success. Phrases such as 'I will have . . .', 'I will be . . .', indicate that what you want lies out there in the future. These future targets may work well for systematic goals, but they do not work well for your creative goals, since you are trying to bring your unconscious on board. This is because the unconscious thinks *only in the present.*

So, write your goal in the present tense, with one important proviso – the statement has to be true! If you affirm something in the present tense that is currently untrue, you sow confusion and doubt in your mind. For example, say someone's goal is to have a fit body weighing 140 lb. So he or she writes, 'I am fit and I weigh 140 lb'. However, what is going through that person's mind as he or she reads this if they currently cannot climb the stairs and weigh 180 lb? That person looks in the mirror and thinks, 'But this just isn't true!' This conflict reduces the possibility of achieving the goal. There are ways around this dilemma, using words that are true. The person could say:

- I want to be fit and weigh 140 lb.

- It is now October 2009 [a point in the near future] and I am fit and weigh 140 lb.

- I am in the process of becoming fit and weighing 140 lb.

Of the three, I prefer the words, 'I am in the process of . . .' Not only is it true now and for any individual goal, it is always true. You are always in the process of living your life, and when you do it proactively, you are in the process of living the life you want. It's a powerful and empowering thought and the words are powerfully true as well.

There is another variation on this. You could pick some point in the future when your goal is achieved and describe what you have achieved in the present tense. For example in

2000 I affirmed: 'It is summer 2001 and Eleanor and I have just moved into our new home in Union Hall. The 2,200-square-foot house looks over Blind Harbour and features a vegetable garden, landscaped grounds and an orchard. In addition . . .' And I added a full description in the present tense. We did actually achieve this in 2001, although the landscaping and veggie garden took a little longer.

RESPONSIBLE

Who is responsible for achieving your goal? Is it you or someone else? Consistent goal-achievers take 100 per cent responsibility for achieving their goals. Of course they usually enlist the help of other people, but they do not totally depend on other people. When the results are negative, the goal-achiever does not blame other people or outside circumstances. (In fact one of the only benefits of not taking 100 per cent responsibility for your goal is that you can blame someone or something for not achieving your goal.) Taking *total* responsibility engenders *total* commitment and persistence, vital factors in goal achievement.

TOWARDS WHAT I WANT

Expressing your goal in the positive is a must. The goal focus must be on where you want to be (positive) not on where you do not want to be (negative). Think about it. If you *want* to be in Dublin, but you state your goal as 'I don't want to be in London', what are you going to focus on? This is not only confusing for your conscious mind, but it plays havoc with your unconscious, because your unconscious cannot process a negative. Close your eyes for a moment and say, 'Don't think of a red bus.' What pops into your mind? A red bus. Now remember that your unconscious will identify opportunities for the goal you communicate to it. It does not distinguish between a positive and a negative. So if you state your goals in the negative (what you do not want) the likelihood is that you will get more of what you do not want.

Having said that, writing down what you *do not* want can be an invaluable tool in goal-setting – provided you then change the statement into what you *do* want.

GOAL-SETTING PROCESS 2:

MY LIKES AND DISLIKES

🖾 Make two columns.

🖾 In the first column write down things you do not want and things you do not like about your current situation.

🖾 Then in the second column reword them to make them things you do want and do like. These positive 'wants' should be included in the description of your goal.

Things I do not like or want	Things I like and want
I don't want to be in London	I want to be in Cork
I don't like dishonest people	I like honest people
I don't like not having enough money	I want plenty of money [then specify how much]
I don't want to be fat	I want to weigh 140 lb
I don't want to live here	I want to live in x, y, or z
I don't like that colour	I want to paint it blue

Table 5

🖾 In addition to utilising the SMART process, try to incorporate goal-enhancing words and language when writing your goal, for instance:

I have decided . . .

This is a strong way of expressing commitment, belief and personal responsibility for achieving your goal. For example: 'I have decided to buy a house in Dingle', or 'I have decided to improve my relationship with my son'. This last statement certainly worked for me.

Words that express positive feelings

These give an amazing positive energy to your goals. Look at the difference between: 'I want a large house in the countryside', and 'I am so excited and happy about the thought of my ideal house in the beautiful countryside'. Or even, 'I love how it feels when I look at the plans for my ideal home in the beautiful countryside'.

So get some feeling into your written goal. Use words such as 'deeply satisfied', 'happy', 'fulfilled', 'love', 'excited', 'over the moon', 'feel good', 'magic', 'amazing', and so on.

DOES MY GOAL NEED TO BE TIMED?

There are two schools of thought: some people believe that it is absolutely essential to put a time – date, year and month – on achieving your goal. It is commonly said that 'a goal without a deadline is just a dream'. Other people maintain that it is totally unnecessary to put deadlines on goals. They believe that when you express your goal clearly and specifically, it will happen in its own time – in other words, when the time is 'right'. I have thought long and hard about this and I believe that, in principle, the more certain you are about *how* to achieve your goal the more realistic it is to set a definite deadline. A goal that lends itself to a specific deadline usually emerges from systematic planning – both fixed and responsive. Because you are clear about the steps you need to take, it is possible and desirable to put completion dates (deadlines) on these goals. For example:

- ☞Building a house or making anything mechanical (Systematic Fixed Goals).

- ☞Sailing from Cork to Bordeaux (Systematic Responsive Goal).

The picture changes, I believe, when the steps towards your goal are less clear or not clear at all. This happens with systematic flexible and creative goals. In many cases it is difficult to put a definite deadline on these types of goal and to actually believe that you will achieve the goal by the given deadline. Many or most of the steps are unknown before you begin and they are also largely outside of your control. Since experience seems to indicate that deadlines are not important for this type of goal, here is what I suggest:

1. Develop a very strong desire for the goal, using all of the techniques described above.

2. Get a feeling for how urgent the goal is: do you want it achieved as soon as possible, or can it happen in its own time?

I came across precisely this time dilemma about fifteen years ago when I was talking with Denis Brosnan, chief executive of the Kerry Group (see Chapter 3). We were discussing how the company project teams set goals: deadlines were always put in place, but there were many examples of projects moving beyond these. Denis was comfortable with this and he explained it this way: 'I believe in always setting a definite deadline. This focuses people. If you have not achieved the goal by the deadline, it means you did not allocate enough time initially. So set a new deadline and stay focused on the goal.'

Another interesting detail in the Kerry Group strategic

planning process is that the company rank all their projects and goals in terms of priority. Time and resources were allocated to the most important goals, which were prioritised and given a strong sense of urgency. So perhaps I could add a third point to my approach:

3. Prioritise your goals according to what is most important to you.

If you adopt this approach you will automatically allocate more time and resources to prioritised goals. This, in turn, generally means they will happen sooner rather than later.

W^2: Describing where you are now

This is a fairly straightforward exercise. You have developed a clear, detailed, specific description of your goal (W^1), so now you can describe, in detail, where you are now in relation to your goal. This description will mirror the description you have of your goal.

GOAL-SETTING PROCESS 3:

WHERE DO I WANT TO BE AND WHERE AM I NOW?

W¹: Where do I want to be?	W²: Where am I now?
I want to be in Dublin.	I am in London, which is 300 miles from Dublin (225 over land and 75 by sea).
I want to build a business that delivers a cash surplus of €50,000 a year.	Last year my business threw off a cash surplus of €10,000. However, the year before it lost €5,000.
I want to be in a serious relationship within two years.	I am currently single and dating no-one. I have had two serious partners in the past.
I want to spend more time with my children.	My life at the moment revolves around the business. I usually work ten-hour days, six days a week. I get home and all I really want is something to eat, to sit down and relax and then to go to bed. Sometimes we go out as a family on Sunday and I take two weeks' holiday every year and the odd weekend off.

Table 6

I am sure you notice, after you have read both columns, the lack of specificity in the first column - especially the last three goals. This clearly demonstrates that the Three W Process is what precisely what it says – only a process. In these examples, there will be continuous movement between **W¹** and **W²** and back again as you become clearer and clearer about where you want to be and where you are now: detail and specificity will begin to emerge.

W³: What am I going to do to get where I want to be?

GOAL-SETTING PROCESS 4:
WHAT KIND OF GOAL AM I SETTING?

- Look at the description of your goal.
- Visualise it. Imagine it has already happened and that you have achieved your goal.

Goal Category	Characteristics of W³	W³: Actions to Take
Systematic Fixed	All steps known and clearly defined	Start with step 1 and keep going – simple.
Systematic Responsive	Steps known, but can change because of changing circumstances.	1. Take step (action) 2. Monitor results (feedback) 3. Take next step
Systematic Flexible	Steps unknown	1. Take small action towards goal 2. Monitor results (feedback) 3. Take next action based on feedback
Creative	Steps can be broadly known or totally unknown	Follow actions for Systematic Flexible and also bring your unconscious and the universal unconscious into play.

Table 7

> 📖 Now take pen and paper and list all the things that happened in order to succeed. This exercise will help you decide whether your goal is systematic or creative and you can see from Table 7 why this is important:

The actions you take to achieve your goal depend on the category it is in. For example, if you are erecting a fence you can list all the actions clearly at the outset and so this falls under the 'systematic fixed' category. At the other end of the scale lies a creative goal. A good example would be a goal I set for myself in 2005 when I said, 'I want to introduce life skills into the curriculum of secondary schools'. I had no idea how or when I was going to achieve this goal. However, over the next twelve months, a series of unexpected events occurred that led to a life skills programme being introduced to three schools in West Cork. All I did was to keep my goal in mind and avail of these opportunities as they appeared – perfect creative goal-setting and 'follow-through'.

What Else Can I do to Maximise the Probability of Achieving My Goals?

There are a number of other add-on steps that you can take to further improve your goal-achievement abilities and skills.

Tackle positive and negative beliefs about your goal
Sometimes our first reactions when we think of a goal include the following: 'Oh, I couldn't do that'; or, 'There's no way that will happen'; or even, 'It sounds good, but I'm not so sure . . .' Doubt and lack of belief are great goal-killers. Using the words, 'I've decided' is an excellent first step. Here are some questions you can ask yourself to build belief into your goals:

- Is this goal achievable? Think in general terms: is it within the realms of possibility and has it been achieved before?

- Is this goal achievable for me? Work with what you think is realistic for you, not what others mean when they say, 'Oh, come on be realistic!' These people are negative – they are goal-killers.

- What degree of certainty do I have that I can achieve this goal?

- What degree of certainty do I have that this goal will be achieved?

- The answers to the last two should be 100 per cent.

For example, say my goal is to climb the four highest peaks in Ireland's four provinces in 48 hours. Is it achievable? Yes, of course it is: many people have completed the 'Four-Peaks Challenge'. But my friends may say, 'Come on Con, be realistic. Think of your age and fitness.' I work it through: 1) People of my age and older have climbed the four peaks; 2) I can work on my fitness and set up a backup team. So yes, it is an achievable goal for me. And, if I set it as a goal, I am 100 per cent certain that I can and will achieve it.

The path to your goals

BALANCE
This means setting goals in all your important areas of life – family, health, career, finance, and so on. Certainly, there are times when you need to make a huge effort in one area; make this a finite period. When you are successfully achieving your goals in this area refocus on the other areas. Balance is essential

to a happy life. We will cover this in more detail in the next chapter.

CONSEQUENCES

Every goal you set and every action you take has consequences – for yourself, others and the environment. At a personal level, goals in one area affect other areas of life – positively and negatively. What will be the consequences of your goal for other people in your life, for the community, for society? When you examine the consequences of your goals, they should at least have a neutral impact. Better again: they should have a positive impact, especially in the other areas of your life and for the people close to you. Ensure that your goals have 'win-win' outcomes.

PERSONAL LEARNING JOURNAL

Use your PLJ to write down everything about your goals: your thoughts about them; the progress you make; the results achieved – successful or otherwise; what happened on the road to your goal; and examples of luck and coincidences that helped you. Your PLJ will reinforce your belief in the goal-achievement process. When you embrace the full Life Planning Process, your life will be driven by setting and achieving goals in the important areas of your life. Your PLJ will become a very inspiring record of your life.

VISUALISATION

Think regularly about your goal. Your thoughts can be based on any of the five senses: seeing, hearing, feeling, smelling and touching. They can also be 'self-talk': describing the goal to yourself. Visualisation keeps your goal in focus and makes it more real to you. It inspires commitment and perseverance.

DAILY REMINDERS

There are many ways to keep your immediate goals in focus:

- Read them before you go to sleep at night.

- Put them on small laminated cards that you can carry with you.

- Pin them up so you face them as you work.

- Record them on your iPod and listen to them.

- Set up a 'goal file' and put in any newspaper cuttings and other information that relate to your goal.

READ ABOUT GOALS

There are plenty of books about goal-achievement and goal-achievers. Some are listed in the appendices at the end of this book. Read about people who have been successful at achieving their goals in all areas of life, from Henry Ford, to Gandhi, to Nelson Mandela.

NETWORK WITH GOAL-ACHIEVERS

Put this another way: network with positive people, because positive people are generally good at setting and achieving goals. Develop some of the practices described in *The Luck Factor* by Richard Wiseman:

- maximise your chance opportunities by networking;

- be curious and open to new experiences;

- listen to your 'gut feelings' and take steps to boost your intuition;

- expect good luck by persisting in your attempts to achieve challenging goals;

- and look on the positive side of negative results.

Now you have a powerful goal-achieving process in place – namely the Three Ws Process. The next step is to get some goals to work with.

CHAPTER 12

FINDING YOUR GOALS

IF ONE ADVANCES CONFIDENTLY IN THE DIRECTION OF HIS
DREAMS, AND ENDEAVOURS TO LIVE THE LIFE THAT HE HAS
IMAGINED, HE WILL MEET WITH SUCCESS UNEXPECTED IN
COMMON HOURS.

(HENRY DAVID THOREAU)

This chapter is particularly exciting because this is where you select the goals that will give you happiness, meaning and success in life. These three words are important – happiness, meaning and success – we will call them HMS. So let's start looking for goals that will provide you with a large measure of HMS. Your objective is to discover what's important to you in life (meaning, purpose) and dedicate your LifeTime to these important 'things' by setting and achieving goals in these areas. The goals you select give meaning and purpose to your life – and lead ultimately to happiness.

This is going to take some time and work – it is not just a matter of selecting some goals this week and then sitting back and enjoying the results. This is an ongoing process. This is life lived to the full. As a first step, I would like you to get your Personal Learning Journal and devote a few pages to the following step-by-step exercises. When you are finished, you will have selected and written down a number of short- and long-term goals. And you will know how to do this as often as you like into the future.

Measuring Your Overall Happiness

Life is all about happiness – when you have meaning and success in your life, you are happy. You can call happiness by other names – contentment, fulfilment, or satisfaction perhaps. Whatever you call it, at the end of the day it's what we all aspire to. We have already agreed that we need some means of measurement to see if we are reaching our goals and since happiness is the ultimate goal, let's put a happiness-measurement system in place. It can be difficult to measure happiness directly, so I use a measure called 'life satisfaction' score. The first exercise helps you assess your happiness score.

SELF-ASSESSMENT PROCESS 8:

LIFE SATISFACTION SCORING CHART

🖜 Copy the table below into your PLJ. For this exercise you will be putting a a satisfaction score on your current level of happiness and contentment in life on a scale of 0–10, where 0 is no satisfaction at all or total misery, and 10 is 100 per cent satisfaction with life, or total happiness.

🖜 While you are deciding on your score, remember to think about your whole life: work, home life, finances, relationships, and so on. Then choose a figure that seems right to you, a figure that you are comfortable with.

🖜 Enter your score in the first column, second row,

directly under the place where you have written today's date.

🖐 Keep monitoring your progress and insert your new scores over the months ahead – there are columns for 3 months ahead, 6 months ahead, 9 months ahead and a year ahead, but you can obviously carry on keeping score for as long as you like.

🖐 Make sure that you add the actual date of the assessment at the top of each column when you write down your score.

Today	+ 3 months	+ 6 months	+9 months	+ 1 year
[date]	[date]	[date]	[date]	[date]

Table 8: Overall life satisfaction score
Score 0–10, where 0 = totally dissatisfied/unhappy and 10 = completely satisfied/happy

🖐 Next describe the life that would give you a score of 10. In other words, a description of your ideal life where you would be totally happy and satisfied. Again write that into your PLJ.

🖐 Now it's time to set some simple, short-term goals. Ask yourself, 'What three actions and decisions will I take in the next two weeks to increase my Life Satisfaction Score by 0.5 of a point? Write these three actions down in a list, numbered one to three.

🖐 Schedule these actions and decisions into your diary.

This exercise includes some of the fundamentals of life planning and time management:

1. You have described your ideal life – the Big Goal.

2. You have chosen some actions to move you towards your Big Goal.

3. You have decided when to carry out these actions.

I hope that you find this a very simple system that you could easily adopt and that provides a good introduction to goal-setting. Next, an even better process that will ensure that you set goals in ways that ensure you have a **balanced life**.

The Balanced Goal-Setting Process

GOAL-SETTING PROCESS 5:

CHOOSING YOUR GOALS

There are ten steps to this process.

1. **decide** on the most important areas of your life (AoLs);

2. **prioritise** these areas;

3. **score** your current level of satisfaction in each area;

4. **ask yourself** if your life is well-balanced;

5. **select** up to three areas of life in which to set goals;

6. **use the three Ws** to set goals;

7. **schedule** the actions needed to achieve these goals into your diary;

8. '**walk** the talk': carry out the actions;

9. **measure** your progress regularly; and

10. **continue** to set goals to lift satisfaction scores in all
    areas of life in order to achieve a balanced happy life.

Write down the list and record your thoughts on each as you
work through the detailed explanations of what each step
involves.

Decide which are the most important areas of your life
What's important in your life? Write down the areas of your life
(AoLs) that you think are important. On my courses, people
usually choose some, or all, of the following:

- family;
- money;
- friends;
- career/work;
- health;
- hobbies;
- fun and recreation;
- socialising;
- personal growth;
- spirituality/religion;
- living environment;
- contribution to society;
- sport;
- involvement in your community.

So make out your list and be as specific as possible. For example,
instead of 'sport', you may want to write rugby or hillwalking.
Or perhaps you want to describe the actual hobby you enjoy –

for instance I would write 'gardening'. Then you may have a specific community interest such as membership of the Lions or the parish committee.

Before you finalise your list, I want to make two suggestions. Firstly, what do you mean by family? People usually say it's the children, spouse or partner and perhaps parents and siblings. But it is worth being far more specific, since I believe that if a person includes their spouse with the children and calls this total relationship the 'family' relationship, this can cause problems. This is because the relationship you want to have with a spouse is different, in many respects, to the relationship you have with your children. Many people do not realise this. Before children arrive there is a single relationship between two people in love. Once children arrive, the tendency is to focus on the relationships with the children and assume that the 'family relationship' covers everything. This often results in neglect of the husband-wife relationship. Suddenly one day the children are gone and two strangers wake up alongside each other in the bed. So, my first suggestion is to separate out your spouse from your children and your wider family and friends. These are separate areas of life.

The second piece of advice involves setting goals in an area of life that we seldom think about = the things we would love to do given the opportunity. Very often these are activities we thought of as young people before we took on life's responsibilities: career, marriage, children, mortgage, and so on. The dreams of our youth get submerged and forgotten when we are facing the realities of life. I have heard these dreams described variously as Dreams, 'Wow' goals or BHAGS ('big hairy audacious goals'). Recently, I came across a very useful down=to=earth example in my own life.

I had arranged to meet my friend Arthur for a day's work on a project. Friday arrived = but no Arthur. To be fair, he had phoned to say he could not make it and rearranged the day's work for Monday. So Monday arrived – and Arthur too – with an unusual explanation: 'Something came up that was on my "bucket list" so I just couldn't turn it down.'

'Your bucket list?' I was mystified. Arthur expanded: 'Well, you see, I have this list of things that I really want to do before I kick the bucket. So I call it my "bucket list".' Brilliant, I had never heard it put so simply. So, I suggest that you include 'Bucket List' as an area of life – but you could just as easily call this area 'Dreams', 'Wow' or 'BHAGS'.

Prioritise these areas.
So now you have a list of your important areas of life. But some are obviously more important than others. Let's prioritise them. You could do this by simply labelling them 1, 2, 3, and so on. However, here's a very emotive approach that graphically brings home to you which areas of your life are really most important. Here's what you do.

Firstly count your AoLs. You should have at least ten. Now I want you to use your imagination and think of each AoL as something you carry in a suitcase. Say you have twelve AoLs and you have twelve suitcases. Now imagine you are emigrating and you take your twelve AoL suitcases to the airport where a small two-engine aircraft awaits you. It's just you, the pilot and your suitcases containing everything that's important to you in life.

The pilot looks at your luggage and says, 'Sorry, this plane can carry only ten suitcases. I'm afraid you'll have to leave the excess behind.' You leave two (or whatever number over ten) behind and load the remaining ten suitcases into the luggage compartment, strap in alongside the pilot, and take off. Make sure you number those you have left behind, starting with 11 and using as many numbers after that as you need.

Your destination is 3,000 miles away across the Atlantic Ocean. Shortly after take-off the pilot notices that temperatures have plummeted and ice is forming on the wings. 'We've got to ditch some luggage or else we'll go down,' he says. 'You must throw out two cases to keep us flying. Now! Go for it!' In your mind's eye, throw out two cases – quickly. Then look at your list and label these 10 and 9. You have eight AoLs left.

That may have been a little difficult, but it gets worse when the pilot urgently announces, 'Sorry about this but it appears that they didn't fill the tanks to maximum, so we haven't enough fuel. We must lighten the load or we'll crash into the sea. Quickly throw out two more cases – now!' Again, look at your list and mentally ditch two, labelling them 8 and 7. This was tougher to do than the first time and you have six left.

You settle back in your seat as the plane flies on and then one of the engines begins to stutter and conks out. By now you know what's coming next. 'We're in trouble again – get rid of two cases – immediately.' No need for explanations, just select two, throw them overboard, and label them 6 and 5 on your list. You now have four precious AoL cases left and your heart sinks when you next hear the pilot scream, 'There's fog at the airport and we're diverted a further 50 miles. We're nearly out of fuel and flying on one engine. Throw out one case and do it quickly. Now! Just do it!' Do it, and label this case 4.

Was that easy? No, it was not! As I know only too well from the experiences of hundreds of people who have attempted this exercise. It is difficult because the exercise forces you, consciously and unconsciously, to define what's really important to you. At this stage you are left with three AoLs that are not numbered. I will not ask you to throw out any of these because these really are the most important areas of your life and I find that it distresses people to choose which to abandon next. This is because the top three always include spouse/partner and children.

Now look at your list. Take some time to reflect on what you see and how you prioritised them. Write your thoughts down in your PLJ. What are the most important things in your life? Where did money come in? What about job or career? What else strikes you? Write it down. This is a very important exercise that teaches you a good deal about yourself.

Score your current level of satisfaction in each area
Your next job is to copy the following table (without my examples) into your PLJ and transfer your AoLs into the table in order of importance. Then put a satisfaction score on each one, just as you did earlier for your life overall. Insert your scores in the 'today' column.

SELF-ASSESSMENT PROCESS 9:

AOL SATISFACTION RATINGS

📖 Ask yourself how satisfied you are with your current level of happiness and contentment in each area of your life on a scale of 0–10, where 0 is totally dissatisfied and miserable, and 10 is completely satisfied and utterly happy.

📖 Make sure you actually write your partner or spouse's name in the space provided.

📖 Each time you add a score to your chart, make sure you put the actual date under 'today', + 3 months, + 6 months, and so on.

📖 Reflect on your scores and write down any comments beneath your chart.

Ranking	Area of Life	Satisfaction Score			
		Today [date]	+3 months [date]	+6 months [date]	+1 year [date]
1	partner (by name)	4			
2	children (by name)	6.5			
3	health	3			
4	our home	7.5			
5	money	8			
6	personal growth	3.5			
7	friends	6.5			
8	career	9			
9	socialising	8.5			
10	Bucket List	2			

Table 9   Average   5.85

In the example above, things are not very good in the priority AoLs – the scores given for partner and children. The score of 4 for the partner indicates potentially serious relationship issues. The score for health is also alarming. On the other hand the scores for money and career are very high. What kind of a life do you think this person is leading? What do your own scores telling you about your lifestyle?

How balanced is your life?

This is a crucial question and it can only be answered when you have pinpointed the important areas of your life and assessed how satisfied you are in each one. Now that your have done this, you can go on to use the Wheel of Life, which gives you a visual representation of the balance between all your most important areas of life and will really drive home the lessons you learnt when you rated your satisfaction in each AoL.

SELF-ASSESSMENT PROCESS 10:

THE WHEEL OF LIFE

1. Draw a large circle in pencil, leaving enough room around the outside of the circumference to write in the names of your AoLs.

2. Divide the circle into segments, one segment for each AoL. Look at figure 3, on which I have allocated ten segments for ten different AoLs. You may have fewer or more AoLs on your own Wheel of Life.

3. Set up your scoring system, with the centre of the circle on each segment representing 0 and the circumference representing 10. Label each segment of the circle with a different AoL (see figure 4).

4. Take a coloured pen or pencil and draw a slightly curved line – echoing the circle's circumference – in each segment to represent the score you gave it in your AoL table, which you have already produced (see figure 5).

5. Finally, join up all the curved lines to complete your Wheel of Life (figure 6).

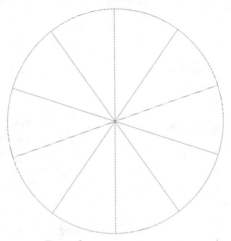

Figure 3

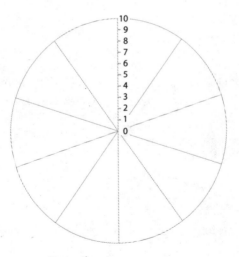

Figure 4

Figure 5

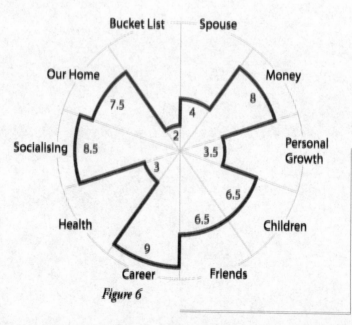

Figure 6

What you have just drawn is your life as a kind of pie chart. Look at the lines you have connected. If your life were a wheel, how smoothly would it be travelling? Look especially at the priority areas of your life. How close to the rim are their score lines? In the example I have given, the person's partner and health are close to the axle of the wheel, with money and career near the rim. What's going to happen to this wheel = to this person's life = if he or she makes no changes? Examine and reflect on your own wheel carefully. What are the messages you are getting? Write your thoughts in your PLJ.

Your Wheel of Life is an excellent way of assessing the balance in your life, especially in the most important AoLs. It is a marvellous tool to help you lift your satisfaction scores (sat score) in a targeted way.

Ideally your wheel should be full and smooth, especially for the top three or four AoLs. A full wheel represents a 'smooth' life, in which you achieve a high degree of happiness and satisfaction in the most important areas. A jagged wheel indicates lack of balance and rough ride through life.

Select three areas of life in which you want to set goals
Over time, you will set goals in all your AoLs, but when you start just select the three that need urgent attention. These are not necessarily the three with the lowest sat scores. Look at how you ranked your AoLs on the table. Move down and select those you think you most need to work on. The sat score is a good indication.

In the detailed AoL satisfaction table we looked at earlier in this chapter (Self-assessment Process 9, focusing on AoL satisfaction ratings), the AoL with the lowest score was the Bucket List (2.0), followed by health (3.0), personal growth (3.5), and partner (4.0). The two more important AoLs are partner and health, so I would select these two to work on. I would also focus on children, although they have a score of 6.5. What I have done is to use both the actual scores and the ranking of the AoLs to choose the areas that need attention first.

After you have selected the three AoLs you want to target, move on to the next exercise.

Use the Three Ws Process to set goals
For this exercise you will be referring back to Chapter 9 as you consider each one of your three targeted AoLs in the light of the three Ws.

GOAL-SETTING PROCESS 6:
SETTING GOALS

W¹: Where do I want to be? Describe, using the information in Chapter 9, your ideal situation for each of your three AoLs. In other words, what your life would look like in these areas if you achieved a score of 10. These are big, big goals, so give it your best shot, take your time and use the SMART process (see Chapter 11) to make these goals specific and measurable. Express them in the present tense and in very positive language, taking 100 per cent responsibility for achieving the goal.

W²: Where am I now? Explain, with as much detail as possible, why you have allocated your current scores: you are trying to paint a picture of your current situation in this AoL. Re-read your explanations and fill in more detail, if necessary, so that your picture is accurate. This exercise will help identify short-term goals and actions, for the next step.

W³: What will I do when I get where I want to be? Some of the steps you need to take will be obvious and some will only appear as you begin to take some action – again, I suggest that you re-

read Chapter 9. However, and this is very important, you must set some short-term goals and take some action very soon. This process is like a snowball. It may be small, but get it rolling and it will gather momentum and get bigger. So too with the Three Ws Process: once you start it, it will bring results, small at first, but getting bigger and better as time goes on.

If you are a little stuck while you are doing this exercise, ask yourself this question: 'What action can I take this week to lift my sat score in this AoL by half a point or more?' If your mind remains blank, take time out, do something else, sleep on it. The answers will come and you will discover a few actions or short-term goals that you can schedule.

Schedule the actions to achieve the goals
When are you going to do what you have decided to do? Whether it's to make that phone call, book that flight, meet that person for coffee; join that club, sign up for that course, or invest in those shares – all the small goals and actions that will move your life along in ways that increase your sat scores in the important areas of your life.

All you need is some sort of diary or time-management system into which you enter the actions you are going to take. Then, when the day pops up in your diary, you just do it.

'Walk the talk'
This one-liner is self-explanatory. When the day and hour arrives, simply make that call; board that plane; turn up for coffee; turn up at the club, sign up for that course; or buy those shares. Whatever actions you have decided to take – take them! It's really very simple at the end of the day. Your life is made up of all the little things you do every minute, hour and day. All you have decided to do is to select the actions that will help you

actively create *your life*. The Eiffel Tower is made up of millions of nuts, bolts, rivets and pieces of iron, each one fitting delicately together, according to a design that produced a magnificent monument in Paris. The large jigsaw you had as a child was made up of a thousand pieces. The picture on the box was the grand design – just as your vision of your future is a map for your ideal life. With patience, skill and judgement you can painstakingly put the pieces together in small daily actions that complete the jigsaw of your life.

Measure progress regularly

As the jigsaw comes together it's easy to see that you are gradually succeeding. It is very visual. You see the corners, edges and different parts of a varied landscape growing before your eyes and, by comparing them with the picture on the box, you know that eventually you will complete the jigsaw. This is the way you measure progress when you are using the Three Ws approach – small local increments that produce the bigger picture.

Progress is easy to measure in the jigsaw. In real life it may not always be as obvious. Progress may be measured clearly if you invest €10,000 in shares – you check their value on the stock market reports. If your goal is to weigh 160 lb, you measure progress on the weighing scales and adjust diet and exercise accordingly. It is easy to measure something when you can put figures on it. But what about your relationships with family and friends; how you feel about your living environment or your career; your assessment of the contribution you make to your community; or the steps you take to grow as a person? You cannot use a calculator, measuring tape or weighing scales, but you do have your own internal measuring system. It's that feeling of satisfaction, which I have called the AoL 'satisfaction scoring' system. Strange as it may seem, you will know when your relationship with your spouse is improving or getting worse. Also with the level of satisfaction you get from friendships, where you live, and your own personal growth.

You started the ball rolling when you measured your levels of satisfaction in each area of your life. In the 'today' column you now have a set of sat scores that reflect your current level of satisfaction in each area. After that you set some goals and took the actions in the three areas of life that most urgently needed improvement. Make sure you revisit your satisfaction scoring chart in three months and fill in your sat scores in the next column to see how you are progressing.

In fact, when you copy the table into your PLJ, why not put in today's date in the 'today' column and then put the actual dates when you intend go back to your chart, and score your AoLs again over the course of the three, six, nine and twelve months that follow? Then put a note in your diary for all these dates: 'Measure my satisfaction levels in my important areas of life.' On the day that you go back to the chart, make sure that you cover up all the previous scores so that you are not consciously comparing today with the scores you gave three months ago.

I list my AoLs on a card at the back of my PLJ and when the due date arrives, I transfer the list to the next blank page in my PLJ and allocate the sat scores. This avoids comparison with the previous scores, which might influence me when I am giving a new score. The comparison comes next. I have another card with my AoLs and the scores I have given them since I started systematically doing this in August 2004 – from this I can see that the scores have gone up in some areas and down in others. Obviously, when a score goes down, you examine what has happened and then go on to set and take new actions to increase satisfaction.

After you become familiar with the Life Planning Process,

you will find you do not use the original satisfaction scoring chart any more. I do not use it – it is far better when you are comfortable with the process to break your life down into AoLs and work on these individually. However, it is still a good idea to keep an eye on the big picture – your overall satisfaction with life. In my own case, I add up all the sat scores for my different AoLs and divide them by the total number of AoLs to get an average. I find this very useful and below you will find the chart that shows my overall progress since 1996 (I estimated that particular year, since I was not aware of the system at that time). From what you have read of my life experiences in Part One, I'm sure you will see that these sat scores reflect what was happening in my life over that period: I was very down in 1996; pretty good in 2004; followed by two years of decreased life satisfaction in 2005 and 2006. Then I really began to get things right and life is really wonderful right now. Sure, there is room for improvement in some areas – and there is also the possibility that it could get (temporarily) worse in other areas, but the process keeps me on track. It can and *will* do the same for you!

September 1996 (estimate)	2004	2005	2006	2007	2008
5.2	8.7	7.6	7.5	8.4	9.3

Table 10: Average life satisfaction scores for Con Hurley

I must add a word of caution and warning on this measurement system: *You can only use it for yourself.* You cannot compare your sat scores to those of your partner, friends or colleagues. This is because the system is very subjective and individuals differ greatly in their assessment of life satisfaction. So you may score yourself 6.5 for health, while somebody in comparatively worse health may score herself a score of 7.5 and somebody in comparatively better health may score himself 5.5. As they say, 'beauty is in the eye of the beholder', and so is satisfaction scoring.

Continue to set goals that lift satisfaction scores

You now know how to set goals and take actions that lead to a happy and balanced life – in other words a *successful life*. Yes, a successful life! Think about it: you have defined and prioritised what is really important to you and you have started a process that will focus on these important areas. The next big challenge is to extend this process into all areas of your life and to keep the process going with the aid of your PLJ.

The rewards are huge. Just keep repeating steps 6 to 9: set goals; schedule actions; take action; measure your progress. When I first started using this method, I found that I scheduled these activities into my diary as regular tasks. However, as the years have passed, I have found that strategic life planning has become part of me. I do not need to check my list to see which are the most important areas of my life. There has been some re-ordering of priority, of course, but I'm very clear which ones are top of my agenda. And I follow through by devoting most of my time and energy to the most important ones, while maintaining high scores in the others.

Areas of Life: a More Detailed Approach

Just as I broke down the overall life sat score into individual AoL satisfaction scores, so also is it possible to break down each AoL into even smaller components. This is extremely useful when you are trying to make urgent progress in a particular area of your life.

For example, let's say you have given your health a satisfaction score of 3.5 and improvement is urgent. After you have described what a score of 10 would look like in this AoL, you will have a description of your optimum state of health. This is likely to include things like maintaining the right weight for *you*, a healthy diet and some sort of fitness regime – the obvious elements of good health. But more specifics are needed so that you can measure your progress. For instance, what do you mean by diet or fitness? What other factors could you include? Get specialist advice if necessary.

Here, for example, is how I score myself 10 for health: 'I weigh 165 to 170 lb; I am a non-smoker; I exercise aerobically 45 minutes per day, six days a week; I consume fewer than 20 units of alcohol a week; I eat a high-fibre diet with plenty of vegetables and fish; I read and write for three to four hours a day; I have comprehensive health checks every two years; I take no long-term medication; I cope very well with the stresses of life; and, finally, I am very happy in, and with, myself.'

That description, I believe, will enable me to work for long hours in the garden, walk long distances, and maintain an active mind, feel well, and – very importantly – maintain good physical health and mental well-being long into the future.

Relationships

Relationships are another area where it is hugely beneficial to get into more detail, as I pointed out when I was insistent that we should distinguish our spouse from our children when compiling a satisfaction chart. And you can, and perhaps should, go even further. If you stop to consider the possibility that virtually everything we need in life is provided through our relationships with others – love, attention, connection, community, friendship, intimacy and fun, for example – it becomes clear that relationships with others are crucial to satisfy most of our basic needs. It can, therefore, make sense to break relationships down and to give each one a sat score.

Here's an example.

Ranking	Relationship	Sat Score
1	Barbara (wife)	8.0
2	Mary (daughter)	7.5
	Sean (son)	4.5
3	Joan (mother)	9.0
4	Jimmy (father)	4.0
5	Mark (brother)	6.5
	Sheila (sister)	9.0
6	four best friends	8.0
7	aunts and uncles	6.0
8	cousins	6.0
9	neighbours	7.5
10	workmates	9.0
11	the boss	3
Average satisfaction score		8

Table 11: Relationship satisfaction scores for Michael

Overall, in the example above, our hypothetical Michael has a good average sat score for relationships at 8.0. However, just look at the detail. There's obviously a need to improve the relationships with his son Sean (4.5) and his father (4.0). The relationship with his boss is very low at 3.0 and, although he is at the bottom of the pecking order, this relationship could have a significant impact on health and career. So Michael's priorities are to focus on these three relationships, going on to take steps to improve his connection with his son, while assessing his overall career situation and his rapport with his boss.

I came across an interesting situation when I used the relationships exercise with a group. One man came up with a score of 7 for the level of satisfaction he felt with the relationship he had with his wife. Looking back to when they had been married ten years earlier, he reckoned the score then would have been 10. 'Now it is down to 7,' he said. 'If I don't do something maybe it will be down to 4 in ten years' time.' The exercise has made me aware that our relationship is deteriorating.' Based on this reasoning, the man spoke with his wife and has taken steps to focus on improving their relationship.

Career

Let's look at an example that illustrates balancing the key components of your work, career or business. In Chapter 1, I made a list of the things that were essential to ensure I did an excellent job as editor of my section. Then I focused on the items on the list and gave little or no attention to what was not on the list – they were not essential to my work. You can do the same for your work or career. The same is true if you run your own business, whether it is in farming, manufacturing, information technology or any other area. What are the factors that are essential to the success of your business? These are sometimes called the Key Success Indicators (KSIs). Here is simple list for the running of a profitable, grass-based dairy farm:

1. The cows bred for a grazing system display:

   a. high genetic merit;

   b. high sexual fertility; and are

   c. efficient converters of grass to milk.

2. The cows are calved to match the availability of grass.

3. The herd calves over a short period: 90 per cent in six weeks.

4. High-quality grass is in plentiful supply, from calving and throughout the grazing season.

5. Infrastructure is available to optimise labour efficiency: key factors are farm layout and milking facilities.

6. Superb management is essential to put all these elements together.

A good farmer will focus on these essential elements for success, set goals and targets for each one, monitor results and progress, and, provided he is committed and skilful, will end up running a very profitable dairy farm. The same approach holds true for every business.

Maintaining Balance

By following the process I have described in this chapter you will maintain balance in your life. You identify your important areas of life and ensure that you maintain high sat scores in all of them, especially the really important ones. Of course, there will be times when you will focus on some more than others. The classic examples are when a person goes all out to develop a great career, or to make a lot of money for some purpose, or when love takes over and you direct most of your time and attention to your loved one.

During these times of intense focus on one AoL, the other AoLs can, and do, suffer. Many a marriage has foundered on a brilliant career. And health is often the victim of the long hours and effort spent in making money. Problems arise when a person does not realise that they have already achieved their goals: how much money is needed to finance your life, or how much time do you need to put into a career?

This is the trap I fell into after the farm failed in 1983 and I was facing bankruptcy. As I mentioned in Chapter 4, Eleanor was a tower of strength and we pulled back slowly from the financial abyss. I did not know anything about AoLs or life planning back then, but I remember clearly asking myself what were the most important things in my life. I came up with the following answers:

- Eleanor and our marriage;

- our three children;

- my health; and

- my career.

In my head I set goals in all four areas. They were not very clear goals and they were not written down, but I knew that I wanted to have a great relationship and marriage with Eleanor. I also wanted to spend a lot of personal time with our children and I wanted to be fit and healthy. The health aspect of my life was easy: I bought hiking boots, rain gear, a compass and a knapsack. And off I went walking the mountains of Ireland and abroad. We also bought a trailer-tent and the combination of tenting and hiking gave us many happy family holidays and kept me fit and healthy.

Great stuff if I had kept it that way! The goal I set for my career was very clear, although I had not written it down: I wanted to be the best dairying journalist in the world. OK, it sounds like aiming for the moon, but the reality is that there were not many of us in the world. The goal was realistic and I set about achieving it with gusto. Did I achieve it? Well, I believe I did, although there is no independent measurement system in place. However, I paid a huge price for my almost obsessive focus on career. I lost the balance in my life completely as I strove to sustain long hours at work, while still maintaining good marital and family relationships. Something had to give – and it did; my health.

Looking back, I see where I slipped up. I went overboard on career. This would not have happened if I had been using the system I have just outlined: monitoring my important AoLs regularly and setting goals in each to increase sat scores and maintain balance. That's what I do now and I urge you to do the same.

SELF-ASSESSMENT PROCESS 11:

MONITORING PROGRESS

Copy this little chart into your PLJ so that you can keep a check on how you are doing as you continue to use the Three Ws Process in every important area of your life. Write your most important AoLs down the left side and tick each box as you complete that stage in the goal-setting process. It may take a few months to get through them all, but the reward and payback is the creation of the successful and happy life you have imagined for yourself.

Area of Life	W¹: Where do I want to be?	W²: Where am I now?	W³: What will I do to get there?

Table 12

CHAPTER 13

LIVE LONGER, LIVE HEALTHIER

YOU DON'T STOP HAVING FUN WHEN YOU GET OLD. YOU GET
OLD WHEN YOU STOP HAVING FUN.

(ANONYMOUS)

I know that you will already be doing a lot of hard work to set goals in your important areas of life. Now here comes the first reward – and possibly also a pleasant surprise. Look back at the LifeTime chart I asked you to create at the end of Chapter 4 – the one that introduces your PLJ. The purposes of that exercise were to: 1) give you a wake-up call; and 2) to introduce you to the concept of LifeTime Management as distinct from Time Management.

I sincerely hope that you have woken up to the fact that your LifeTime is limited but – and here comes the pleasant surprise – it may not be *quite* as limited as this chart suggests. This chart is based on an average: on average, people die at about eighty years of age in the western world, with men mostly dying under eighty and women over eighty. But just because this average exists it does not mean that you *will* die at around eighty. Let's look at the statistics in a different way - as a LifeTime Graph.

The graph shows that 50 out of every 100 people die before they are eighty and the other 50 die after eighty. This is why

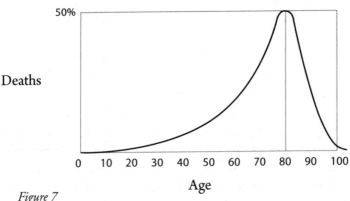

Figure 7

eighty is the average age of death. The key question for you is: which side of eighty do you want to be on? Where do you want to be on the graph? Obviously, like most people, you want to live to a ripe old age in good health and with a good quality of life. By now I imagine you are asking yourself:

- What can I do to lengthen my life?

- What can I do to ensure that I enjoy a healthy, high-quality life into my final months?

Calendar Age, Physical Age and Psychological Age

To help find answers to these questions, I want you to look at age from a different perspective – in fact three different perspectives.

- **Calendar age** is marked off, year by year, from the day you are born.

- **Physical age** is the way your body responds to ageing.

- **Psychological age** is the way your mind responds to ageing.

Generally speaking, we use only one measure of age – that is our **calendar age**. Each birthday we measure our age by counting the years since our birth. The key point with this perspective on ageing is that we have absolutely no direct control over our calendar age. Every year the birthday cards remind us that time moves on remorselessly.

Society and culture also play their part in reinforcing this concept of age: generally our society regards us as 'productive' until we retire at sixty-five or earlier. The perception is that once you retire you become burden on the state – unproductive and useless. It is no wonder that many older people more or less give up and spend their final years waiting to die. Many – but not all.

However if you start looking at ageing from a physical or psychological perspective, you see a different picture. In these areas you can exercise a large degree of personal control and the reward can often be a longer, healthier calendar life.

What is your physical age?
Firstly let's consider **physical age**, meaning the effect of ageing on your body. I'm sure you have often seen two people of the same calendar age and observed how different they are physically. School reunions can be very revealing. Have you, or someone close to you, ever remarked, 'Look at him, he looks twenty years older than the rest of us', or perhaps, 'She'd pass for forty. I wonder what she does to keep herself so young?' These are good questions – apart from cosmetic surgery, what indeed *does* she do to keep young? And what *does* he do to appear older?

Fortunately, there is a growing body of research looking at answers to these questions. Take, for instance, Dr Henry Lodge's ground-breaking book called *Younger Next Year*. The book is co-authored by Chris Crowley, who is living proof that, using Dr Lodge's advice, it is possible to live an active, healthy and long life. Chris exercises for about 1 hour a day, six days a week: he cycles or rows for four days and does yoga and weight-training on another two days. That's the price he pays for being a vibrant, fit, healthy 74-year-old. Is the reward worth the price? Chris certainly thinks so.

Dr Lodge says that: 'Seventy per cent of premature death and ageing is lifestyle related. Heart attacks, strokes, common cancers, diabetes, most falls, fractures and serious injuries, and many more illnesses are caused by the way we live. If we had the will to do it, we could eliminate more than half of all disease in men and women over fifty. Not delay it, eliminate it! This is a readily attainable goal.'

This book is a must-read if you accept responsibility for your health and want to live a long and healthy life. The core message is that you can make a difference if you exercise aerobically every day for 45 minutes, six days a week – for the rest of your life. It sounds simple and also a bit boring and onerous. Imagine committing yourself to 45 minutes every day jogging, swimming, cycling or walking. But why not? The reward is huge.

Taking responsibility for your health means doing whatever it takes to have good health and minimising the practices that damage your health: smoking, a sedentary lifestyle, obesity for example. On my courses, I ask people to make lists of factors that can shorten your life and those that can contribute to a longer, healthier life. These are the suggestions they come up with.

Factors that Can Shorten My Life	Factors that Can Lengthen My Life
Stressful relationships, at work and home	Supportive relationships with people who listen and advise in times of worry. Love, family, friends.
Financial difficulties	Taking responsibility for improving my finances.
Imbalance in work/life ratio	Taking steps to ensure a good work/life balance.
Lack of job satisfaction/reward	Correct career choice: choosing to work in an area that suits my skills and talents, where I feel fulfilled/acknowledged and properly rewarded.
Unproductive worrying about things I cannot change (for example wars, politics, the economy).	Being more easy-going. Not sweating the small stuff and the things I cannot do anything about.
Loneliness and isolation: lack of family/friends.	Being in a career or situation in which my contribution matters. Making sure I have good friends if there is no family.
Feeling disempowered (common in teenage or old age). Alternatively, staying in an unequal relationship or a situation of financial/emotional dependence.	Taking some control over, and responsibility for my life. Taking control of and resolving problems.

Table 13

Factors that Can Shorten My Life	Factors that Can Lengthen My Life
Bad health, mental or physical.	Enjoying good health and maintaining that health with a healthy lifestyle. Eating healthily. Giving up smoking. Regular health monitoring.
The inability to let go of worries and unresolved problems – feelings of bitterness.	Contentment Having a good grip on reality: the ability to accept things I cannot change and the courage to change the things I cannot live with.
Difficult working or living conditions: for example where I have no control over the weather or where equipment is not working efficiently.	Seeing the positive. Feeling empowered to make changes.
Stress	Exercise and other forms of stress release.
Lack of purpose	Creating purposes and setting goals for my life.

Table 13 cont.

The key conclusion here is that taking responsibility for resolving difficult situations in your life and making appropriate lifestyle choices can greatly influence your physical ageing process. While this generally leads to a longer calendar age – you live longer – it also means that your body remains healthier longer. You have a huge influence on whether you end up in a wheelchair or on a bicycle at ninety! Or whether you sit listlessly in a nursing home or walk to the shop for the paper every day.

Will you choose the factors and lifestyle that can bring you a longer, healthier life? I hope you do.

What is your psychological age?

What about your **psychological age**? This is your 'mental' age, how old you feel in your head and also, very importantly, what you can do to feel young mentally. Some of the factors that affect your psychological life are listed in the following table.

Socialise mainly with older people.	Include many younger people and people with a youthful attitude in your social circle.
Socialise mainly with negative people.	Socialise with positive people.
Have a negative approach to life.	Develop a positive mental attitude.
Have disempowering beliefs.	Have empowering beliefs.
Cultivate pessimism.	Develop optimism.

Table 14: Factors that can affect my psychological age

HAPPY NUNS

It is clear that there are many things you can do to develop and maintain a 'younger' mindset. What's the payback? Well, as well as feeling better about yourself, there is evidence that you will live longer on the calendar as well. And we have perfect proof of this fact. In 1932, 180 nuns entered a convent and became part of a long-term study of longevity and happiness. For the rest of their lives the nuns lived and worked in the same environment. They did not smoke or drink, had the same access to good health care, and were in the same social and economic class. However, there were wide variations between how long the nuns lived. The researchers examined how each nun looked at life. The table that follows summarises the results:

	Happiest Nuns 25%	**Unhappiest Nuns** 25%
Alive at 85 years old	90%	34%
Alive at 94 years old	54%	11%

Table 15: Happy nuns

The conclusion is clear – a happy nun is a long-lived nun!

ELDERLY NEW YORKERS

Happiness was also one of the factors identified in a 1973 New York study by Dr Stephen P. Jewett, a psychiatrist, which looked at seventy-nine healthy people of eighty-seven years and older. Jewett identified the powerful positive forces behind the long age and high quality of life of these people. The majority of the factors were psychological, or tied in to their lifestyle and behaviour. They were:

- people who enjoyed life, exhibiting a high degree of optimism and a marked sense of humour. They regarded life as a great adventure;

- mentally active, with a keen interest in current events and good memories;

- relaxed and free from anxiety, experiencing few illnesses, and not prone to worry;

- often self-employed, whether in the professions or farming;

- occupied and did not retire early;

- resilient and, although most had been hit by the Depression in the 1930s, they had recovered and built new futures;

- people who lived in the present, not the past;

- not preoccupied with death;

- often religious, but not extreme in their beliefs;

- moderate eaters, with no special diets;

- all early risers, taking about six to seven hours sleep per night;

- as diverse in their drinking habits as the general population;

- often, but not always, non-smokers or ex-smokers;

- people who used very little medication.

AUSTRALIANS IN RETIREMENT

Next, there's the fascinating study on the quality of life of 200 retired Australians. The study was carried out in the late 1990s by consulting psychologist Michael Longhurst, who asked the question, 'What do happy people do in retirement that unhappy people do not?' Since we already know that happy people live longer, the Australian findings are very significant.

The research team measured how each person had adjusted to retirement by examining their levels of retirement-related:

- anxiety;

- depression;

- stress; and

- satisfaction (happiness) in retirement, compared with life before retirement.

In *The Beginner's Guide to Retirement*, Longhurst describes eight factors that significantly affect happiness and satisfaction in retirement. In my view, these same factors are relevant to any person whether they are retired or not.

1. Being able to retire of your own free will: being in control of your future.

2. Being able to retire at the age of fifty-five or younger allowed those in the study to choose activities and personal challenges while they were still young and healthy enough to do so.

3. Being financially independent: that is, comfort versus subsistence. People who depended on government pensions suffered more depression, anxiety, stress and were less satisfied with life than people who were financially independent.

4. Engaging in 'purposeful activities' for more than five hours a week. Being busy at something that has meaning and purpose such as community work, a new career, and so on. Golf or mowing the lawn were not seen as 'purposeful' activities!

5. Having someone whom they could rely on for emotional support: the availability of a shoulder to cry on. It proved important to maintain relationships with family and friends.

6. Proactively maintaining health through exercise, diet and regular medical check-ups.

7. Planning for retirement: both financially and for an active lifestyle.

8. Receiving pre-retirement advice or education.

PEOPLE WITHOUT PURPOSE DIE YOUNGER

A study was carried out about forty years ago on a group of bank managers who retired at the age of sixty-five. Former manager Jack Cagney, since deceased, communicated the fascinating results of this study to me personally. The study found that 50 per cent of the managers died within one year of retirement and another 25 per cent were dead by the age of sixty-seven. The startling overall result was that three out of four managers (or 75 per cent) died within two years of retirement. But why? The conclusion was that the managers died because they had lost interest in life – they had lost their purpose. While they were actively working for the banks, they had had a respected career, an active social life and a high social standing within the community – all strongly connected with their positions as bank managers. Most of their socialising was associated with their jobs: activities such as membership of a golf club, civic receptions, and so on.

When they retired, most of this disappeared – and, at that stage, without adequate interests and preparation for retirement, most of them died quickly. 'Meaning' and 'purpose' had vanished from their lives with the job.

OPTIMISTS LIVE LONGER

In 1962 scientists at the Mayo Clinic selected 839 patients who had referred themselves for medical care. On admission they each took a series of psychological and physical tests. One of the tests was for optimism. Over thirty years later those still living were again assessed for optimism and the researchers found that optimists lived 19 per cent longer than pessimists.

Conclusion

The studies we have looked at all seem to conclude that we have a huge amount of influence over the quality of our lives, both physically and mentally, and that the way in which we make choices, or exercise this influence, can contribute to a healthier, longer life. Of course there will be accidents and other factors outside your control, but much, if not most, of the quality and length of the rest of your life lies within your control.

CHAPTER 14

LIFETIME MANAGEMENT

YOU CANNOT MANAGE TIME. YOU CAN ONLY MANAGE
YOURSELF. TIME MANAGEMENT IS LIFE MANAGEMENT.

(BRIAN TRACY, *TIME POWER*)

Look at the title of this chapter again. It's not 'time management' or 'lifetime management', it's 'LifeTime Management' with capitals, or LTM for short. There's a good reason for this and Brian Tracy's introduction to this chapter has summed it up well. Moreover, since it is your own life you are managing, LTM is all about self-management. You cannot manage a diary or a clock; you can only manage your self. Remember, we live our lives through the actions we take every minute, hour and day. In Chapter 11, you started the process that is the essence of LTM: you identified what was really important to you in life and you set yourself goals and actions to achieve those goals. You should also have scheduled these actions into your diary or whatever you use for day-to-day time management.

This is what I call proactive LifeTime Management, which I like to sum up using a misquote from Goethe:

I will allocate my time to the things that matter most to me.

Herein lies the essence of effective LTM: simply identify what matters most and give those things all of your time. This is the core principle of life planning, irrespective of what tools or system you use. Get this right and you will find that you are living life the way you want to live it.

Basic Principles

Your LifeTime is invaluable, irreplaceable and finite. How you spend it will determine how successful, happy, contented, fulfilled and productive you are. The following principles of LifeTime Management are all aimed at enabling you to make the best use of your time:

1. **Define the Three Ws in your own life:**

> (i) where you want to be;
>
> (ii) where you are now; and
>
> (iii) what you are going to do to get to where you want to be.

2. **Work on your mission statement** in support of the Three Ws. This is the essential 'big picture', describing you and what's important to you in life. We will look at your Personal Mission Statement in Chapter 17.

3. **Assess your important areas of life.**

Describing these clearly ensures that you incorporate them effectively into your mission statement.

4. **Make strategic decisions and set goals.**

These are the planned choices and decisions you consciously make in the different areas of your life. There should be a close fit (congruence) between these decisions and choices and your mission statement.

5. **Take action.**

This is the 'doing' and 'living' part. Effectively, this is how you spend your time (lifetime). You deliberately choose, on a day-to-day basis, to devote time to taking the steps that will achieve the goals that will enable you to achieve success in the 'important things' in your life.

These principles form a very practical and robust structure for LifeTime Management. However, we must remember that our world is constantly changing. We do not have perfect knowledge of our purpose in life. What you regard as success today may well be different from your definition in five years' time. We are (or should be) constantly growing in self-knowledge. In other words, we are changing as we get to know ourselves better.

Against this reality, LifeTime Management is not an easy or straightforward task. But it must be done. Because if *you* do not manage your lifetime, someone else will. Other people and other circumstances will run your life. Is this what you want?

We must **react** to the changing circumstances by making choices and decisions that fit best with our *current* mission statement and what we believe are the important areas of life – at that moment.

A sixth principle could now be added to the five I have already listed:

6. **Continually review and update** the first five principles.

This final principle takes account of the fact that we are constantly growing and changing, as is the world around us. Our values will rarely, if ever, change. We can develop our strengths. Our role during life will change, as will the ranking of importance in our areas of life. So we must regularly review our mission statement, areas of life and goals. An annual 'mission statement check' is a good idea. Then modify and change your allocation of time accordingly.

LifeTime Management in Practice

There are many ways and systems of organising your time. Different systems work for different people. There is no one right way. It is up to you to select the right system for you, whether it is a calendar, a palmtop organiser or a diary. What works for you is what is right for you. Irrespective of which system of time organisation you choose, there are two key principles that will help you to make the best use of your time. These can be broken into two areas:

1. The 'big picture', or proactive LifeTime Management; and

2. Detailed time organisation – planning weekly and implementing daily.

The 'big picture'

The 'big picture' covers the rest of your life. It means defining the areas and roles that are most important for you and then ensuring that you spend your time in these areas. This is **proactive** time management. Research has shown that successful people plan their lives five, ten and even twenty years into the future. They take a **long time perspective**. They evaluate and choose their actions in the present in terms of how these choices fit with their long-term goals. The longer the time perspective, the more likely you are to make the choices that lead to long-term success.

The LifeTime Chart exercise in Chapter 4 should have focused your mind on the importance of getting the big picture right. Your life is finite. It's up to you to make the best use of it.

Goethe put it well when he said,

Things that matter most should never be at the mercy of things that matter least.

This is the core principle of LifeTime planning, whether in the original or my, perhaps more positive, rendition: 'I will allocate my time to the things that matter most to me.'

Ask yourself what you want out of life. Develop a life strategy – a personal life plan. The whole objective is to decide how you are going to live your lifetime. Your time, or more accurately, your lifetime, is limited. Amazingly, most people live their lives as if they will live forever, continuously deferring important goals until 'next year'. Filling in the LifeTime chart demonstrates forcibly that your life is finite. The implications are clear – we need to make the best possible use of the time that remains to us. LifeTime is a non-renewable resource.

This is a great way of focusing the mind. But on what? That's a question that each individual must answer for him- or herself, but if you are in any doubt, look back to the six principles of LifeTime Management at the beginning of this chapter. These will lead you to your answers:

Detailed time organisation

An interesting way of looking at LifeTime Management is to imagine your life as a 5-gallon bucket. You can fill this with a mixture of rocks: big ones, small ones, pebbles and sand. The big rocks represent the very important things in your life: family, personal development, a successful business, your spouse or partner, and so on. The smaller rocks represent things that are less important, but that you would still like in your life. The pebbles are far less important and the sand represents time-wasters and things that are totally unimportant.

Think of what happens if you fill the bucket without any thought. It will fill up with a mixture of big rocks, small rocks, pebbles and sand. Remember that 'nature abhors a vacuum' Your days and hours will be taken up with something, whether you plan it or not. Your 'bucket of life' will end up half full of sand (unimportant things) and there will be no room for the big rocks – the important things.

It takes a lot of effort and time to empty out some sand and pebbles and make space for the big rocks. Far better to put the big rocks in first and then fill in some of the spaces with smaller rocks and pebbles. You achieve this when you identify what matters most for you – your family, business, and so on – and then go on to allocate time to these areas, set goals and take action. What are your 'big rocks'? You identified them in Chapter 12 when you made a list of the important areas in your life – and you also discovered that some rocks are bigger than others when you ranked them.

The following steps will then help you to effectively organise your time so that you always give enough time to the 'big rocks'.

1. Systematically allocate time to:

    i. the planned steps and tasks that relate to your balanced goals; and

    ii. reviewing your life plan, mission statement and goals.

2. Develop efficient work organisation. Work out simple, effective systems for your job or business, identifying the essentials for optimising efficiency. 'Optimise' may mean 95 per cent effectiveness. Striving for the last 5 per cent may not be worth the time, effort and resources required. Strive for perfection (100 per cent), but settle for excellence (95 per cent).

3. Take time to think before allocating time to requests or work that come at you unexpectedly. Create a 'space'

that allows you to evaluate these tasks against your own plans and mission statement. Then make an informed decision to reject or take on the request or work.

4. Say 'no' to unimportant things.

5. Delegate where possible and appropriate.

6. Identify and eliminate time-wasters and time 'bandits'. Remember Goethe's words and do not allow the 'things' that matter least to steal your time.

7. Focus on the factors within your control.

PLAN WEEKLY, IMPLEMENT DAILY

An effective approach is to allocate planning time to organise your hours in the coming week. Use some form of planning tool, such as a diary. Each week identify the one activity or task you can do in each role or focus area – the one that will make the greatest contribution to achieving each goal. Allocate time for these key tasks. Give your energy and time to the things that produce the greatest results.

SETTING WEEKLY GOALS

Copy the chart below and use it to go through this process:

1. Set aside one hour per week to organise how you spend your time every day.

2. Look at some, or all, of your areas of life and the goals you have set in them. Some may be more important than others at different times.

3. For each one selected, ask this question: 'What is the most important thing I could do this week that would have the greatest positive impact on achieving this goal?'

4. Schedule that thing into your diary.

Area of Life Goal	What is the most important activity I could do this week that would have the greatest positive impact?	Schedule the action

Table 16

THE USE OF TIME ANALYSIS

One approach to finding out how you use your time at present is to carry out a daily time audit. Write out a daily timesheet and fill in whatever you do during the day. Do this each day for a typical week, then work out how much time you spend at various activities. You can use this information to:

☞ calculate how much time is being allocated to your major areas of life and goals;

☞ see how much time is going into the essential work of running the business, and the various activities associated with it;

☞ identify activities that contribute nothing to your goals – the time-wasters and time bandits.

Saying 'no'

I tend to overload my back with my mouth. (Tony Robbins, *Unlimited Power*)

Effective LifeTime Management means saying 'yes' to the things that matter most and 'no' to the things that matter least. This should become a fundamental personal habit. It is also called assertiveness. Learn to say 'no' firmly but politely. Remember that your time is what it says – your time. Nobody else can, or should, take it from you without your permission. Other people's problems may be important and urgent (for them), but you are not required to solve them. So when other people and things are likely to encroach on your time, stand back and evaluate the requests for help against your goals. If there is a fit, then you can answer 'yes' to a request. But if there is no fit, or a poor fit, you can choose to say 'no'.

As Stephen Covey says, 'You have to decide what your highest priorities are and have the courage – pleasantly, smilingly, and non-apologetically – to say 'no' to other things. And the best way to do that is by having a bigger 'yes' burning inside' (*The 7 Habits of Highly Effective People*).

Once, listening to the radio, I heard an interviewer talking to a woman whose family had achieved an enviable balance. She was married to a very busy man who worked long hours and many weekends. Yet they still managed to take adequate family holidays and weekends away as a couple each year. The interviewer asked the woman how they managed this. She told him that she and her husband put great store on their family and their relationship as a couple – and believed in giving both relationships the time they deserved. So, after Christmas each year, they would sit down with two new diaries – his business diary and her personal diary. Then they would decide on the time for the family holidays in the coming year and their weekends to themselves as a couple. Her husband, Jim, would use a red pen and mark these dates in his diary. When he returned to the office in the new year, he would ask his secretary to do the same with his appointments diary and she always knew that these dates were untouchable.

At this point the interviewer asked what happened if something really important came up. The woman answered that if it were absolutely critical for Jim to be at a particular appointment or event, he would swap times – but they would always get their holidays and weekends away. She added that, in practice, this happened very, very seldom, because his colleagues would work around Jim's diary. Also that he never told his colleagues that he was taking a few days in Paris with his wife, or a week in West Cork with the family. No, he would simply say that he would not be available that week and the others would make alternative arrangements.

This is a superb example of prioritising time around what's really important and letting things that are *also* important – but *less* important – find their own time slots.

CIRCLES OF INFLUENCE AND CONCERN
These concepts are important in both proactive and reactive time organisation. Your circle of influence includes those things you can affect directly – things that are within your control to a greater or lesser extent. Your circle of concern comprises all those things that affect you, but are largely outside your control.

Proactive people spend more time and effort on factors within their circles of influence. They expand their knowledge and experience, and their circle of influence grows (see figure 8). Effective time organisers will put time and effort into the factors within their control.

Reactive people focus more on their circle of concern, on factors outside their control. The result is that their circle of concern grows and gains control over them (see figure 9). People in this situation commonly blame all their problems on factors such as the weather, the banks, the political system, and so on. The more time they spend talking and thinking about these factors, the less they can do for themselves.

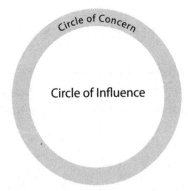

Figure 8

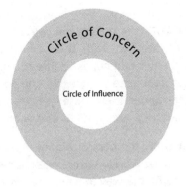

Figure 9

CHAPTER 15

THE INNER YOU

THERE IS FOR EACH MAN A PLACE, WHICH HE IS TO FILL, AND
NO ONE ELSE CAN FILL, SOMETHING WHICH HE IS TO DO,
WHICH NO ONE ELSE CAN DO; IT IS HIS DESTINY!

(FLORENCE SCOVEL-SHINN, *THE GAME OF LIFE AND HOW TO
PLAY IT*)

There are many definitions of the word 'self', because it means different things to different people. Keeping things as simple as possible, I would suggest that there are two essential aspects to self:

1. **The Outer Self**: the person the world sees and the way that person interacts with their environment through their relationships and needs. In the course of our Wealth Creation Courses (see Chapter 3), the participants learn a good deal about their 'outer selves', by working on financial planning, areas of life and goal-setting.

2. **The Inner Self**: the person within, the self that is often invisible to the world. Also one's 'conscious' self or 'reflective' self: the way in which our thought processes work, the values we hold, our emotional needs and our quest for meaning and purpose in life. This is the realm of psychology, life coaching, philosophy, spirituality, religion and many other complex 'mind and spirit' variants.

In my opinion, gaining knowledge of your outer self is relatively easy, since this process focuses almost entirely on conscious, external factors that reflect the way we live our lives. The journey inwards is far more difficult, but in many ways more exciting and more rewarding.

A point of crucial importance is that the inner and outer selves need to be in harmony in order to live a fulfilled, happy, meaningful life. The way we live our lives, everything we do in our outer lives, should ideally reflect our values and emotional and spiritual needs. Balance and integrity are important. When our actions are in conflict with our inner selves the results are unhappiness, disease and emotional distress.

My own search for knowledge of the 'inner me' is proving fascinating, exciting – and difficult. As my New Zealand friend, Lynaire Ryan, puts it: 'The journey inwards is the most difficult of all.' Even so, I strongly believe it is a journey worth starting and continuing, because there are huge rewards in the discovery of one's inner self.

How can we go about gaining knowledge of our 'inner selves'? The remainder of this chapter reflects the work I have been doing in my own life and the lessons I have learnt. It is by no means a blueprint. You may well take a different route and that's fine. Deepak Chopra puts it well:

> In the end we all want the same things. We want to be happy. We want to be fulfilled. We want meaning and purpose in our lives. We want a sense of connection to God and Spirit. We want other people to love and respect us. And we want to feel safe. These desires are universal. But the route each of us takes to satisfy them is uniquely our own. We're all heading for the same destination, but we take different roads. We arrive together having travelled our different paths.
>
> (*SynchroDestiny*)

What Are My Values?

What can you do to start your own inner journey? I'm sure a few thoughts crossed your mind when I asked you to make a list of what's important in your life in Chapter 12. I suggested areas of life that might be appropriate, but I imagine a few other important factors crossed your mind: honesty, freedom, and love, for example. The things we set most store by – the character traits or guiding principles we believe to be worthwhile, desirable or useful – these are the things we call 'values', and every person has their own personal set of values that they aim to live by.

Your values are very much a description of who you are *inside*. And they are a great guide when making difficult decisions. They tell you what's 'right' or 'wrong' about a person or situation – according to *your* standards. Without realising it, you live your life according to your values. And when you feel good about something or someone, it means your values are being met. And when someone or something feels wrong, it means that your values are being challenged. Listen to these feelings. They tell you a lot about your values – and your inner self.

So the first step on your journey inwards is to identify your values. There are two ways to do this: the hard way and the easy way. The easy way is to look at a list of values and select those that you think apply to you. However, the temptation is to select values that you would like to have, or believe you should have. Let's leave the list till later (you will find it rounding off this chapter) and take the harder, but more meaningful, route to begin with. Here are some questions that will help you uncover the values that you use to guide your life. Get out your Personal Learning Journal and use it as you work through the exercise.

SELF-ASSESSMENT PROCESS 12:

AREAS OF LIFE

Examine the list you made of your important areas of life and ask yourself the following questions about each one:

🖙 What's important about this AoL?

🖙 When I make progress in this AoL, what will it give me?

For example my main hobby is vegetable gardening. What, apart from beautiful fresh veggies, does this give me? My answer includes: peace of mind, tranquillity, meditation, creativity and contact with nature. Work through your AoLs and see what values you come up with.

The Goals You Set

You can learn a lot about yourself from the goals you set in life. These can be long-term, short-term, financial or personal. Think of a goal that you have set for yourself and ask yourself:

🖙 Why have I set this goal?

🖙 What will this goal give me?

Begin your answers with words such as: 'so that . . .'; 'in order to . . .'; 'because I will get . . .' This approach should eventually lead you towards recognising the values you hold most deeply. For example, one of my goals is to do forty-five minutes' aerobic walking, six days a week for the rest of my life. I have adopted this habit *because* I believe this will give me fitness and good health and a longer life. The obvious value here is good health, but there are other values, such as taking responsibility for myself, proactive involvement and achievement. Note that I could also use the phrases, 'so that . . .', 'in order to . . .', or 'I will get. . .', and I would come up with the same answers.

The Company You Keep

There's a lot of truth in the old saying, 'Show me your friends and I'll show you yourself'.

> ☞ Think about your friends and other people or groups you enjoy spending time with.

> ☞ Think about the sort of people you would not be seen dead with.

> ☞ What values jump out in each group?

When I think of my closest friends, values such as love, honesty, friendship, courage, loyalty, trust and integrity stand out.

The People and Situations that Make You React

Ask yourself:

> ☞ What qualities of character do I most admire in others?

> ☞ What qualities of character do I most dislike in others?

Again, think of the friends whose company you prefer and those you are not attracted to. Also, think of people and characters in history, books, plays and films. They are a rich source of value discovery.

What exhilarates or upsets you in certain situations? For example, I get extremely angry when I watch *Schindler's List*, a film that tells the story of Oskar Schindler, a businessman who protected and saved the lives of many Jews during the Holocaust. My anger tells me that some of my most important values have been challenged by the images of Nazi activity against the Jews – values such as freedom and respect for human life. Schindler's actions, on the other hand, reveal to me still more personal values that are important to me – empathy, courage, contribution and generosity.

Think of people, events, situations, books, newspaper

articles, films, and so on, that evoke in you strong negative emotions such as anger, hatred, fear and guilt. What does this reaction tell you about yourself? What values are being challenged?

Ask Others to Assess You

Now here's an interesting exercise and definitely not one for the faint-hearted. The idea is that you put together a list of questions about yourself that you want other people to answer. I did this as part of my Life Coaching Diploma and it was very revealing – both about myself and my friends. Devise the questions you want to ask, get a list of up to ten people, ask them if they are willing to participate, and then send them the questions. The answers may surprise you – but they will enlighten you. Here are the questions that I posed to ten people during my diploma course:

- If you were to describe Con's character in one sentence, what would you say and why?

- What do you think Con values most in life?

- What are Con's main talents?

- How could Con improve his relationship with you?

- Are there things that Con does or says that annoy you? Please give some examples and suggestions for change.

- How well does Con handle stress? What could he do to handle it better?

- If you could change three things about Con, what would you change and why?

- When you think of Con, what potential do you think he has in his life?

- What aspects of Con (behaviour, beliefs, habits,

weaknesses, and so on) might be stopping him reaching his full potential?

☞ Name three of Con's strengths and how he uses them best.

Life Experiences

The decisions you have made in the course of your life are a great source of value identification.

☞ Think of times when you felt really upset, angry, worried or tense. These uncomfortable feelings meant that your values were being violated. What values were they?

☞ Think of times when you felt really great – happy, respected, uplifted. What values were being fulfilled and honoured through these positive feelings?

These exercises will give you a list of your values. Well done – you have just taken the harder, but better, way to uncover the values that matter most to you. Now go to the end of the chapter and look at the list of values I have put together. Most of yours will be on the list and there may be a few more you have not thought about. Complete your list.

The next step is to prioritise them – which are your most important values? You can do this using the same exercise that you used to prioritise your AoLs in Chapter 12: the exercise in which you were carrying your most important areas of life in suitcases.

Fundamental Human Needs

Now I want to turn to another aspect of our inner selves – our needs. The idea is that each of us is born with a similar set of basic needs for things such as survival, love and security. Our needs are mainly satisfied through the relationships we have with others and with ourselves. The extent to which our basic needs are positively satisfied has a huge bearing on our ultimate happiness, as well as our health – mental and physical.

Your needs are a huge part of the 'inner you', so I believe it is important to gain an increased understanding of them. On my own journey inwards, I have found that the published work of Abraham Maslow, William Glasser, and Joe Griffin and Ivan Tyrell has helped me greatly in my understanding of what *exactly* human need is. As you read through the following theories and descriptions of human needs, distilled from their writings, think about how these ideas relate to your own needs and values.

Understanding human needs

In 1954 an American psychologist called Abraham Maslow started a revolution in psychology and psychiatry when he published a controversial book, *Motivation and Personality*. In it he advanced a new theory of human motivation that challenged some of orthodox psychology's most basic concepts. Maslow based his theory on his study of individuals he believed to be outstanding, rather than the study of emotionally disturbed individuals, statistical averages, or rats and pigeons. From his observation of those people who he termed 'self-actualised', he concluded that the entire human species has common and apparently unchanging psychological needs. These needs provide the framework for common human values.

Our needs are part of the core essence of who we are, and the extent to which our needs are satisfied has a huge influence on the state of our emotional well-being: whether we are happy or sad, and whether we are totally sane or suicidal. It was for this reason that Maslow described a spectrum of human emotional well-being, as it relates to the fulfilment of basic human needs. Translating Maslow's idea to a scale of my own, running from minus 5 to plus 5, it becomes clear that the individual's position on the spectrum influences both their physical and mental well-being.

- The 'normal' state of well-being is situated around zero. That's where most people are; doing fairly well, neither too happy nor too sad.

- As you move towards minus 5, people are suffering increasingly from emotional and mental distress. Their human needs are not being met.

- As you move towards plus 5, you will begin to meet people who are very happy and emotionally strong. Their needs are being met.

Before Maslow published his ideas, psychologists had based their theories and therapies on the clinical study of individuals who would have fallen on the minus side of my scale for emotional well-being: the emotionally unwell and mentally ill. Maslow was very scathing of this approach and said, 'It becomes more and more clear that the study of the [mentally] crippled, stunted, immature and unhealthy specimens can yield only a cripple psychology and a cripple philosophy'.

Think of an analogy based on farming and business. If you want to succeed in either, do you concentrate totally on the study of low-profit farms and businesses? If you want to solve fertility problems in a dairy herd, do you seek out the herds with the biggest fertility problems to find the secrets of good fertility? Of course not, but that was what psychologists were doing until Maslow came along. It is sad to note that many of today's researchers and practitioners still adhere to the '400 variations of cripple psychology' (a statistic cited by Griffin and Tyrell) that Maslow exposed over fifty years ago.

Maslow first published his 'hierarchy of human needs', or keys to emotional well-being, in a paper called 'The Theory of Human Motivation', but during the 1960s the psychiatrist William Glasser picked up the trail in his book *Choice Theory*, expanding Maslow's ideas and identifying five basic human needs. More recently, in 2004, Joe Griffin and Joe Tyrell published their ground-breaking work, *Human Givens*, which catalogues a far more detailed range of human need.

All these men concluded that our needs are very much a part of our inner selves and that we are all born with a similar set of basic human needs – a need for survival, a need for love, a need for security. Our needs are mainly satisfied through the relationships we have with others and with ourselves. The extent to which our basic needs are positively satisfied has a huge bearing on our ultimate happiness as well as our health – mental and physical.

As you read through the three descriptions of human need that follow, think of their relevance to your own life and record your thoughts in your Personal Learning Journal. Think about what needs are being satisfied or thwarted in your different areas of life. Remember also that one of your major life goals is to bring out the best in *you*, to endeavour to become all that *you* can be: this occurs as you realise your talents by fulfilling your needs and moving towards plus 5 on Maslow's emotional well-being scale. Is this the ultimate in self-leadership?

Maslow's hierarchy of human needs

According to Maslow, human nature consists of a hierarchy of needs, which are genetic in origin and unchanging. He believed that these needs are *weak*, in the sense that many individuals never discover them. But that they are, at the same time, *strong*, since if they remain unfulfilled this causes emotional disturbance. Maslow identified five levels of human need that everyone must recognise in their search for satisfaction and happiness:

1. **Physiological Needs:** oxygen, food, water and a relatively constant body temperature, achieved through adequate shelter. These biological needs are the strongest, since they are to do with basic survival – an individual must be able to survive before considering higher levels of need.

2. **Safety Needs:** physical security, in other words safety from wild animals, extremes of temperature, criminal assault, murder, chaos, tyranny and war. Thankfully, most people in the developed world live in fairly safe environments that cater for their safety needs.

3. **Belongingness and Love Needs:** love, acceptance, being part of a group. Generally achieved through external relationships with others, this need involves giving, as well as receiving, love and affection.

4. **Esteem Needs:** both self-esteem and the esteem a person gets from others. This need involves recognition, feeling worthwhile and being respected. Humans have a deep need for a stable, firmly based, high level of self-respect and respect from others.

5. Maslow describes this as a person's need to be and do that which the person was 'born to do'. Even if all the other needs are satisfied, a person can still be discontented and restless if he or she is not doing what he or she is fitted for. As Maslow puts it, 'Musicians must make music, artists must paint, poets must write if they are to be ultimately at peace with themselves. What humans *can* be they *must* be. They must be true to their nature.'

Maslow portrayed his five basic needs as a triangle. In figure 10

I have adjusted this slightly to form a pillar shape, which I think shows more clearly the relationship between the five. It is obvious, as Maslow emphasised, that the bottom needs must be satisfied before a person can move on to satisfy the higher needs – the physiological and security needs are like an essential foundation before you can erect the pillars of love and esteem. Then, once the pillars of love and esteem are in place, a person can pursue their destiny (nature) and self-actualise at whatever they were meant to be. To me, that is happiness – the roof of the temple of life. I believe the route to actualisation is through personal growth and self-knowledge.

Figure 10

William Glasser

In *Choice Theory* William Glasser wrote that there are five needs programmed into our genes and that, from birth, we all try to satisfy these needs through the relationships we have with others. His five needs are:

🖙 survival

🖙 love and belonging

- fun and creativity
- power
- freedom

Analysing Glasser's list more carefully, we see that survival is a purely physical need; the next four are emotional needs, with freedom also taking in self-actualisation (in other words, we need to be 'free' to become what we are capable of). In terms of self-knowledge and the 'inner you', Glasser's main contribution is his understanding that we all satisfy our needs, especially the emotional ones, through our relationships.

His theory therefore underlines the importance of relationships in our lives. When you think about it, we live most of our lives through and with the relationships we have with others – spouse or partner, children, family, work colleagues, community and wider society. And it is through these relationships that we satisfy our needs – for love, power, fun, and so on. We manage our relationships through our behaviour and, consciously or unconsciously, we have total choice over the behaviours we use. Freedom comes when we realise that the only behaviour we can control and influence is our own, rather than the behaviours of those we relate to and interact with.

Glasser also wrote about the way in which strength of need varies from individual to individual. For example, one person may have a strong need for power and will be driven to control others. Another may have a weak need for survival and will be willing to take more risks than someone with a greater need for survival. Particularly interesting is Glasser's outline for what he believed were the level of needs most likely to lead to a successful marriage. As you read his lists, just think of what can happen in a marriage where one person has a high need for power and the other's need is low. Or when someone has a high need for freedom, in contrast to the other's lesser need.

Need	Level in the Best Marriage
survival	average
power	low
love and belonging	high
freedom	low
fun	high

Table 17

Griffin and Tyrell

According to *Human Givens*, we are programmed from birth to fulfil certain physical and emotional needs. Griffin and Tyrell list our physical needs as:

🖙 air to breathe;

🖙 drinking water;

🖙 nutritious food;

🖙 enough sleep to dream;

🖙 freedom to stimulate our senses and exercise our muscles; and

🖙 secure shelter where we can grow, reproduce and bring up our young.

However, the main focus of the book is on our emotional needs. These are, as Griffin and Tyrell perceive them:

🖙 **security** – safe territory and an environment that allows us to develop fully;

🖙 **attention** – the opportunity to give it and receive it;

🖙 **a sense of autonomy** and control;

- an emotional connection to others;

- the perception that one is part of a wider community;

- friendship and intimacy;

- a sense of status within social groupings;

- a sense of competence and achievement;

- meaning and purpose, which come from being stretched in what we do [create] and think.

It seems obvious to me that our emotional needs are mostly to do with the relationships we have with ourselves and with others. These relationships start in the womb and continue after birth, playing a huge role in the way in which our emotional needs are met and how we develop emotionally and mentally. Much of this is involuntary: we have no control over who our parents are, their behaviour, where we live, other family members, where we go to school, and so on. When we are young, therefore, we are conditioned largely by our environment and the relationships within it. When we do go on to exercise control by making our own choices and decisions, we try to meet our innate emotional needs (human givens) through our conditioned choices, actions and behaviour. Therein lies the kernel of emotional distress, mental distress (illness) and aberrant behaviour.

Griffin and Tyrell believe that we must all be aware of, and use, what they describe as the resources given to us by nature, since these resources offer solutions and tools for living life and meeting our needs in an emotionally healthy way. According to Griffin and Tyrell, the key resources inherited by all humans include:

- the ability to develop a complex long-term memory, which enables us to add to our innate knowledge and to learn;

- the ability to build rapport, empathise and connect with others;

- imagination, which enables us to focus our attention away from our emotions and solve problems more creatively and objectively;

- a conscious, rational mind that can check our emotions, analyse and plan (a function of the brain's left hemisphere);

- the ability to 'know' or to understand the world unconsciously through metaphorical pattern-matching (a function of the brain's right hemisphere);

- an observing self – that part of us that can step back, be more objective, and recognise itself as a unique centre of awareness, apart from intellect, emotion and conditioning (a function of the brain's frontal lobes); and

- a 'dreaming' brain that preserves the integrity of our genetic inheritance every night, by metaphorically defusing emotionally disturbing expectations not acted out the previous day.

I admit that all this may look a bit heavy – and I have to confess that I am still reading and re-reading *Human Givens* to get to grips with the ideas developed by Joe and Ivan. It's all part of my journey into my 'inner self'.

Your Path to Self-Actualisation

We have looked at the concept of values in this chapter in order to help and encourage you to look *into* yourself and to consider where your values come *from*. Based on my own reading, I would suggest that our values may well be derived from our genetically programmed needs and modified by the environment we have been brought up in from birth. This, I hasten to add, is only my opinion. But it may help to explain how human beings can share a common set of values, while at the same time differing so very widely in the values they actually *display* in life.

The understanding of this whole area may be difficult and challenging – moreover it is a journey only you can make, on your own. But the reward will be self-knowledge, leading to Maslow's concept of self-actualisation. And surely that is the ultimate reward of your path – to know and become what you were meant to be. So read widely, discuss these concepts with others, reflect and, above all, record your thoughts in your Personal Learning Journal.

Honesty	Truth	Friendship
Integrity	Spirituality	Assisting others
Peace of mind	Creativity	Innovation
Humour	Independence	Romance
Contribution	Joy	Perseverance
Autonomy	Risk-taking	Playfulness
Adventure	Vitality	Security
Love	Trust	Self-reliance
Achievement	Fairness	Simplicity
Success	Excellence	Problem-solving
Ambition	Courage	Wisdom
Openness	Dignity	Respect
Beauty	Excitement	Empathy
Community	Fulfilment	Responsibility
Freedom	Fun	Connectedness
Harmony	Balance	Contentment

Table 18: Human Values – those things which we perceive to be worthwhile, desirable, or useful to human beings

CHAPTER 16

QUESTIONS ARE THE ANSWER

QUESTIONS ARE UNDENIABLY A MAGIC TOOL THAT ALLOWS THE
GENIE IN OUR MINDS TO MEET OUR WISHES.

(ANTHONY ROBBINS, *AWAKEN THE GIANT WITHIN*)

This is a very unusual chapter because you are going to do virtually all the work. I have put together a list of questions and I am going to sit back while you answer them – and it's up to you to *commit* to answering them. I will not be reading your answers and allocating marks.

These questions are designed to encourage and help you to think about yourself and the answers will be of huge value when you come to the next chapter. Please give them the time and reflection they deserve. I suggest that you select the questions you want to answer first – not necessarily in the order I have given them. Then copy the first question into your Personal Learning Journal and write your answer. Move on to the next question, and so on, until you have completed them all. You may find it difficult to come up with some answers. If so, leave the question in your mind and do something else. Take a walk, do some work or sleep on it. You will usually find that answers will come.

Try to give an answer to all questions even if you think some of them are repetitive. Leave some space in your PLJ between each question and your answer, because you may well want to add more to your answer later. Take your time – a week or two sounds about right.

PERSONAL MISSION STATEMENT 1

1. What is my definition of success in life?

2. If I had unlimited time and resources, what would I choose to do? For example, what would I do if I won €15 million in the lottery?

3. When I look at my work life, which activities and roles do I consider of greatest worth?

4. When I look at my personal life, which activities and roles do I consider of greatest worth?

5. Imagine you are on your deathbed. You are peaceful and not in pain. You are able to think clearly. Now come back to today and ask yourself what you need to do, be and have in your life *right now* to ensure that in the future you can say, 'I am dying happy.'

     i. Make a list of all the reasons you are dying happy.

     ii. Then write, 'I am dying happy because . . . [complete in detail].'

6. Imagine a rich relative has died and left you an annual income of £100,000 (increasing with inflation) for the rest of your life. The *only* condition is that you must work at something on a regular basis. You can choose to work at whatever you like. What would you choose and why?

7. Imagine you are totally alone. You have nothing except yourself – no family, friends, work, clothes, possessions, money, knowledge, hobbies, skills – nothing except

yourself. From where you stand alone you have a clear vision of the world around you. You can select anything from that world to make you successful. Try to select those things that you think are absolutely essential for your success in life. Now, list *what* you would choose and *why*.

8. Imagine you have met your guardian angel (or genie) who says to you, 'You have the power to be and do whatever you want to be and do, and I will help you use your power to make it happen.' What will you say to your guardian angel or genie?

9. You go to the doctor who tells you that you have six months to live:

    i. What is your reaction?

    ii. What do you do for your final six months?

    iii. Ask yourself, 'Are there things I feel I really should do, even though I might have dismissed such thoughts before for various reasons?' What are the things you feel that you really ought to do?

10. If you knew that you were going to die in the morning, what regrets would you have?

11. What would you do if you knew that you could not fail? Imagine it! You cannot fail! Write down what you would do.

12. Make a list of the things you want more than anything else. Your 'wants' may be tangible possessions (house, farm, and so on) or they may be intangible (happy family, friendship, and so on).

13. Make a list of the things that you *must* have in order to have lived a successful life.

14. The coffin is in the church. Your body is in the coffin and you are looking down on it. Important people from your lifetime (living or dead) come to the pulpit to talk about you and your life.

    i. What people would you like to come up to say 'goodbye' at your coffin?

    ii. What would you like each person to say about you? Write down what they say.

15. You are going to a wonderful restaurant for a meal. You can invite five people, living or dead, historical or fictional, to dine with you.

    i. Name the five people.

    ii. Describe why you invited each person.

    iii. What does this tell you about yourself?

16. Think back on your life to times when you were totally exhilarated, when time seemed to stand still.

    i. What was happening?

    ii. What does this tell you about yourself?

17. What do I consider my most important contributions to others?

18. What talents do I have, whether developed or undeveloped?

19. Identify three things in your life that are of *great importance* to you. For each ask:

    i. What is important to me about that?

    ii. What does it give me?

      iii. Ask the same questions again for every *answer* that you give. Keep going until you run out of answers. What is left?

20. What do you currently think your life purpose is?

21. What gives meaning to your life?

22. Read this statement: 'When I die I will meet the person I might have been.' Think about it and describe 'the person I might have been.' What does this tell you about yourself?

23. You have applied for a job that you really want: it could even be your present occupation. The prospective employer knows that you can do the job from your qualifications, but he or she is trying to find out what sort of person you are, so they ask that old interview classic: 'What personal attributes and characteristics do you have that will make you a suitable person for this job?' Write down your answer.

Well done – you now have a huge amount of insightful information about your own character and values in your PLJ. This will be of immense benefit to you in the next chapter as you put it all together.

CHAPTER 17

PUTTING IT ALL TOGETHER

WE SHOULD KNOW WHAT OUR CONVICTIONS ARE AND STAND
FOR THEM. UPON ONE'S OWN PHILOSOPHY, CONSCIOUS OR
UNCONSCIOUS, DEPENDS ONE'S ULTIMATE INTERPRETATION OF
FACTS. THEREFORE IT IS WISE TO BE AS CLEAR AS POSSIBLE
ABOUT ONE'S SUBJECTIVE PRINCIPLES. AS THE MAN IS, SO WILL
BE HIS ULTIMATE TRUTH.

(CARL JUNG)

This is a another deceptively short chapter because, once again, you are the one doing the thinking and the writing. You are now ready to construct your Personal Mission Statement by addressing some of the core questions of self-knowledge as outlined in Chapter 2. I say you are 'ready', although I do not know what stage you are at to tackle these fundamental questions of life. Neither, I suspect, do you! However, you have to start somewhere and sometime. Give the answers your best shot.

Below are four statements that I would like you to complete in your Personal Learning Journal. You will find it helpful to read back over what you have already written as you worked through *Yes I Can*. You will find that you continue adding information and refining these statements for the rest of your life. This is the never-ending journey of self knowledge.

To help you get started, I would like to recap what I have already written about self-knowledge. In my opinion, self-knowledge (and arriving at the key components of a Personal Mission Statement) means:

1. describing who I am physically, mentally and spiritually – my **identity**;

2. knowing what's really important to me in life – also my **identity**;

3. doing the best I can to achieve the things that are really important to me – **success**;

4. discovering my ultimate purpose or meaning in life – my **purpose**.

Take time to put your statements together and consult the entries you have already made in your PLJ. For instance, your AoLs tell you an awful lot about what's important to you and this will help you define what success and purpose mean for you. Read over Chapters 5 to 8 again in order to consider the question, 'Who am I?' And study carefully the answers you gave to the questions in Chapter 16. You have a huge amount of information in your PLJ, both from the questions you have answered and the thoughts you have recorded. It's all coming together.

PERSONAL MISSION STATEMENT 2

Write down and complete the following statements in your PLJ:

I am ....
....
What's really important to me is..................................
....

My purpose in life is..
....
Success for me means..
....

You have now taken the first steps towards self-knowledge. You can see that it's not just about reading books. That helps, of course, but it's up to you to do the real work and, as I said earlier, the payback is immense. The statements you have just written provide you with the personal equivalent of a Business Mission Statement. You are developing your own Personal Mission Statement.

Are you giving it the time it deserves? Remember, that the most successful businesses devote serious human and financial resources to this crucial aspect of strategic management. Think about the amount of time and effort you put into the following:

- buying a new house;

- getting an education;

- planning a holiday;

- running a business; and

- training for a job or career.

You have already demonstrated the ability and commitment to devote whatever is needed to be successful in these aspects of your life. The question for you now is: 'Will I allocate the necessary time and resources to what, ultimately, is the most important journey in life?' I hope your answer is a big 'yes'! Good luck and get writing in your PLJ.

To laugh often and much; to win the respect of intelligent people and the affection of children; to earn the appreciation of honest critics and endure the betrayal of false friends; to

appreciate beauty; to find the best in others; to leave the world a bit better, whether by a healthy child, a garden patch, or a redeemed social condition; to know that even one life has breathed easier because you lived. This is to have succeeded (Ralph Waldo Emerson).

EPILOGUE:

WHERE NEXT?

Congratulations and thank you for reading *Yes I Can*. I sincerely hope that my experiences and the lessons I have learnt will help you on your own journey of self-discovery. The promise of *Yes I Can* was to provide you with a life planning toolkit that would enable you to create personal success – happiness – in your life. I wanted to get you to understand and define the important areas of your life and then to take steps to increase your satisfaction scores in each area. As a result of setting these focused goals you will increase your levels of happiness in life.

So, where do we go from here? Yes, I said 'we' because I believe that we will all benefit if more people decide to focus on what is really important in life and become happier as a result. In fact, the whole world will be a happier place to live in; that's really where this book is leading to. And it needs your help to turn Yes I Can into Yes We Can! So, if you want to make more people happy and the world a happier place, this is what I'd like you to do:

- Spread the word about *Yes I Can*. Encourage your friends and relations to buy the book and do the exercises.

- You can download free copies of all the exercises in *Yes I Can* from my website www.conhurley.com. Use them yourself and give them to your friends.

☞ You can make a much, much bigger impact by doing the interactive exercises on my website. The more people that participate, the more information we will have about what really makes people happy.

This information can be used by you, your friends and me to encourage the institutions in society to put more measurement and resources into the pursuit of human happiness instead of the blind pursuit of economic growth. Get me right, economic growth is important, but not as important as the key components of happiness – close, loving relationships, marriage, children, family, friends and health.

Readers and friends, think of this as the start of a movement – the 'happiness movement'. Join with me and others on www.conhurley.com to make the world a happier, better place for all of us, now and into the future.

APPENDICES

APPENDIX 1: THE LUCK FACTOR

APPENDIX 2: RECOMMENDED READING AND CONTACTS

APPENDIX 1:

THE LUCK FACTOR

How do you explain people who just seem to achieve their goals through luck, good fortune, coincidence, and so on? Professor Richard Wiseman of Hereford University posed that question in an eight-year study on hundreds of 'lucky' and 'unlucky' people. He concluded that 'lucky people, without realising it, use four basic principles to create good fortune in their lives'. Note his use of the word *create*. He found that so-called 'lucky' people were not born lucky. Wiseman further concluded, and proved, that you can control and increase your luck. In other words you can become more and more successful at achieving your goals. I strongly urge you to read *The Luck Factor*. Here is a distilled version of his four basic 'luck principles'.

Principle One: Maximise Your Chance Opportunities

- ☞ Build and maintain a strong network of luck by interaction with many people. The more people you meet, the higher the chances that you will come across opportunities – or that they will come to you.

- ☞ Be curious and relaxed about life. You are surrounded by opportunities, which can be a mixed blessing if you are too focused. See what is *there* rather than what you *expect* to be there.

Be open to new experiences in your life.

Principle Two: Listen to your 'Lucky' Hunches

Listen to and trust your 'gut' feelings and other feelings.

Take steps to boost your intuition. Meditation works.

Principle Three: Expect Good Luck

Set challenging goals that are achievable and expect good luck to help you fulfil them.

Attempt to achieve your goals, even if your chances of success seem slim.

Persevere in the face of failure.

Expect your interactions with others to be lucky and successful.

Visualise good fortune.

Principle Four: Turn Bad Luck into Good Luck

Look on the positive side of your bad luck.

Remember that the ill-fortune in your life may work out for the best.

Do not dwell on your ill-fortune.

Take constructive steps to prevent more bad luck in the future.

APPENDIX 2:

RECOMMENDED READING AND CONTACTS

References by Chapter

Chapter 1: What Makes Me Tick?

Charlesworth, Edward A., & Nathan, Ronald G., *Stress Management* (London, Souvenir Press, 1982).

Chapter 3: Self-Discovery

Covey, Stephen, *The 7 Habits of Highly Effective People* (London, Simon & Schuster, 1992).

Covey, Stephen, *The 7 Habits of Highly Effective Teens* (New York, Fireside, 1998).

Lynch, Dr Terry, *Beyond Prozac: Healing Mental Suffering Without Drugs* (Dublin, Marino Books, 2001).

Whitworth L., Kimsey-House H., & Sandahl P., *Co-Active Coaching: New Skills for Coaching People Towards Success in Work and Life* (California, Davies-Black Publishing, 1998).

Chapter 5: Who is Responsible for My Life?

Frankl, Viktor, *One Man's Search for Meaning* (New York, Washington Press, 1984).

Chapter 8: Attitude Determines Your Life

Andreas, Steve, & Faulkner, Charles, NLP: *The New Technology of Achievement* (New York, HarperCollins, 1994).

Easterbrook, Gregg, *The Progress Paradox* (New York, Random House, 2003).

Ellis, Dave, *Creating Your Future* (New York, Houghton Mifflin, 1998).

Keller, Jeff, *Attitude is Everything* (Tampa, INTI Publishing, 1999).

Robbins, Anthony, *Unlimited Power* (London, Pocket Books, 2001).

Robbins, Anthony, *Awaken the Giant Within* (New York, Fireside, 1992).

Chapter 9: The Strategic Life Planning Process

Berman Fortgang, Laura, *Living Your Best Life* (London, Thorsons, 2001).

Byrne, Rhonda, *The Secret* (book and DVD) (London, Simon & Schuster, 2006).

Ellis, Dave, *Creating Your Future* (New York, Houghton Mifflin, 1998).

Losier, Michael, *The Law of Attraction: The Secret behind the Secret* (London, Hodder & Stoughton, 2007).

Wiseman, Richard, *The Luck Factor* (London, Arrow Books, 2004).

Chapter 13: Live Longer, Live Healthier

Chopra, Deepak, *Ageless Body – Timeless Mind* (London, Rider, 1993).

Lodge, Dr Henry, & Crowley, Chris, *Younger Next Year: Live Strong, Fit and Healthy – Until You're 80 and Beyond* (London, Time Warner, 2005).

Longhurst, Michael, *The Beginner's Guide to Retirement* (Dublin, Newleaf, 2000).

Chapter 14: LifeTime Management

Covey, Stephen, Merrill, Roger, & Merrill, Rebecca, *First Things First* (New York, Simon & Schuster, 1994).

Tracy, Brian, *Time Power* (New York, AMACOM Books, 2004).

Chapter 15: The Inner You

Glasser, William, *Choice Theory* (New York, HarperPerennial, 1999).

Griffin, Joe, & Tyrell, Ivan, *Human Givens* (East Sussex, HG Publishing, 2003).

Maslow, Abraham, *Motivation and Personality* (New Jersey, Addison-Wesley, 1987).

Scovel-Shinn, Florence, *The Game of Life and How to Play It* (1st edn USA, 1925; London, Vermilion, 2005).

Further Reading

Berman Fortgang, Laura, *Take Yourself to the Top* (London, Thorsons, 1999).

Butler-Bowden, Tom, *50 Self-Help Classics* (London, Nicholas Brealey Publishing, 2007).

Chopra, Deepak, *SynchroDestiny* (London, Rider, 2003).

Elkin, Bruce, *Simplicity and Success: Creating the Life You Long For* (Victoria, BC, Trafford, 2003).

Fritz, Robert, *The Path of Least Resistance: Learning to Become the Creative Force in Your Own Life* (New York, Fawcett, 1989).

Handy, Charles, *The Hungry Spirit* (London, Arrow, 1998).

Johnson, Spencer, & Blanchard, Kenneth, *Who Moved My Cheese?* (London, Vermilion, 1999).

Martin, Paul, *Making Happy People* (London, Fourth Estate, 2005).

Ricard, Mattieu, *Happiness* (London, Atlantic Books, 2007).

Tracy, Brian, *Maximum Achievement* (New York, Fireside, 1995).

Contacts

Independent life coaches
Boylan, Ann (life and leadership coach & trainer):
    www.carpediemcoaching.ie or carpediemcoaching@ireland.ie;
    Tel. 00353 (0)86 8367317.
Coleman, Bernadette (career coach):
    Website, www.careerwisecoaching.ie;
    Bernadette@careerwisecoaching.ie.
Dalton, Greg (job & career coach):
    Website, www.jobnet.ie; greg@jobnet.ie;
    Tel. 00353 (0)1 2606000.
McCullough, Barry (One of the elders in the 'global tribe of artists'
exploring new ways of living, working and prospering as an Artist):
    www.thekitchentableartist.com
Silfverberg, Julie (life coach):
    Website, www.successpartners.ie;
    Julie@successpartners.ie.
Zantingh, Mety (life and confidence coach):
    Website, www.colourandcoachingforconfidence.com;
    mezamy@iol.ie.

Life Coaching Organisations
European Mentoring and Coaching Council provides information on coaching organisations and coaches throughout Europe.
    Website: www.emccouncil.org.
Irish Coaching Development Network is developing an independent framework for the development and accreditation of life and business coaching in Ireland.
    Website: www.icdn.ie.
Life and Business Coaching Association of Ireland is the regulatory and supervisory body that governs the profession of life and business coaching. Contact them for a list of accredited coaches, training organisations and workshops.
    Website: www.lbcai.ie.